The Role of US Diplomacy in the
Lead-Up to the Six Day War

To
my granddaughters Lia and Hadar
and my grandson, Omer

The Role of US Diplomacy in the

Lead-Up to the Six Day War

Balancing Moral Commitments and National Interests

ZAKI SHALOM

sussex
ACADEMIC
PRESS
Brighton • Portland • Toronto

2 4 6 8 10 9 7 5 3 1

First published 2012 in Great Britain by
SUSSEX ACADEMIC PRESS
PO Box 139, Eastbourne BN24 9BP

and in the United States of America by
SUSSEX ACADEMIC PRESS
920 NE 58th Ave   Suite 300
Portland, Oregon 97213-3786

and in Canada by
SUSSEX ACADEMIC PRESS (CANADA)
8000 Bathurst Street, Unit 1, PO Box 30010, Vaughan, Ontario L4J 0C6

British Library Cataloguing in Publication Data
A CIP catalogue record for this book is available from the British Library.

Library of Congress Cataloging-in-Publication Data
Shalom, Zaki.
[Diplomatyah be-tsel milhamah. English]
The role of US diplomacy in the lead-up to the Six Day War : balancing moral commitments and national interests / Zaki Shalom.
p. cm.
Includes bibliographical references and index.
ISBN 978-1-84519-468-0 (h/b : alk. paper)
   1. Israel–Arab War, 1967—Diplomatic history. 2. Egypt—Military relations—Israel. 3. Israel—Military relations—Egypt. 4. United States—Foreign relations—Israel. 5. Israel—Foreign relations—United States. 6. Israel—History—1948–1967. I. Title.
DS127.2.S5313 2012
956.04'6—dc23

2011032282

Typeset & designed by Sussex Academic Press, Brighton & Eastbourne.
Printed by TJ International, Padstow, Cornwall.
Printed on acid-free paper.

Contents

Acknowledgments

It is my pleasure to thank those who assisted me in preparing this book for publication. First, I wish to extend my gratitude to my assistant, Ms. Jacqueline Snowsky, who spent many hours in reading the text and suggesting corrections, both to the content and the language. I would like to thank my former student, Dr. Boaz Vanetik, who read the book and suggested helpful changes. It is also my pleasure to thank Prof. Rivka Carmi, President of Ben-Gurion University, Prof. Zvi Hacohen, Rector of Ben-Gurion University, and Prof. David Newman, Dean of the Faculty of Humanities and Social Sciences at Ben-Gurion University, for arranging the grants needed for publication of the book. Last but not least my heartfelt gratitude goes to the staff at the Ben-Gurion Research Institute: Ms. Michal Mouyal, Head of Administration, Ms. Bat Sheva Ben Shimon, Coordinator for Purchasing, Adi Moskovich, former Head of Office at the Institute and Sigalit Elcabir Cohen, present Head of Office at the Institute. My thanks also to Ms. Lili Adar Head of the Library, Mr. Yefim Magarill, librarian, Ms. Hana Pinshow, Head of the Archives, Ms. Liana Feldman, Archivist, and Mr. Yosef Litus and Morris Levi from the Computation Unit, who offered assistance whenever I needed computer support.

The Role of US
Diplomacy in the
Lead-Up to the Six Day War

1

Israeli–Syrian Relations
Historical Background

In the years before the Six Day War, Syria adopted a radically hostile policy toward Israel. Following the 1956 Sinai Campaign, the Syrian border became Israel's most volatile region and the focus of daily security operations. Israel was at a loss to find an efficient means of deterring Syrian activity. This was by no means an easy task for Israel, as Syria enjoyed an undeniable topographical superiority over Israel due to its control of the Golan Heights. The weapons that Israel possessed at that time substantially limited its ability to damage Syrian strongholds on the Heights.

Theoretically, sending infantry units to charge fortified positions on the Golan mountain was a viable military option to cope with the Syrian threat. However, this strategy posed significant risks, which would entail a high number of casualties among the attacking forces. Alternatively, the Israeli Air Force (IAF) could attack from the air, neutralizing the Syrians' sense of superiority. Israeli leaders, foremost among them the Prime Minister/Defense Minister, David Ben-Gurion, essentially refused to allow the use of the air force on daily security operations, preferring to hold them in reserve for special occasions. Levi Eshkol, who replaced Ben-Gurion in mid 1963, adopted and enforced this doctrine, though less vigorously.

For years, Israel was hesitant and highly cautious in its military policy towards Syria. Israel's leaders could not rule out the possibility that Syria's reaction to the Israeli Defense Forces' (IDF) activity would be brutal. It was highly reasonable to expect that Syria would choose to direct its fire against civilian targets, rather than undertaking the risk of confrontation with the IDF. This meant that the civilian settlements beneath the Heights would become easy and vulnerable targets of Syrian retaliation.

Furthermore, Israel was deterred from acting against Syria by political constraints that could not be ignored. The hostile activity being directed against Israel was generally local and sporadic, and by its nature received little worldwide attention. Israel, on the other hand, had to respond with relatively large forces. These punitive raids usually resulted in a high number of casualties. Naturally these events came to the international community's attention and were harshly criticized. Israel, at this period of time, was a weak state politically and economically, and much dependent on the international community. It was highly susceptible to international criticism.

Syria, as well as other Arab states, was well aware of this weakness. Under such circumstances, it is understandable that Syria's military activity was carried out with a strong dose of self-confidence. The hostile acts against Israel grew increasingly instigative, demonstrating Syria's willingness to risk wider cycles of confrontation.

Israeli military and political analysts observed that Damascus' impudence stemmed primarily from its historical experience with Israel. Unlike other Arab states that had been involved in armed clashes with Israel, Syria had been spared the trauma of humiliating defeat at the hands of Israel. Had Syria suffered such a setback, it was argued, it might have been deterred from its provocative activity against Israel. An outstanding expression of this perspective was Israel's failure to force Syria to accept Israeli sovereignty over all of the land it acquired after the War of 1948.

Eventually – as an integral part of the Armistice Agreement with Syria – Israel was obliged to agree to a vaguely formulated arrangement based on demilitarized zones. The arrangement's wording left room for contradictory interpretations by both parties. Israel claimed that it had been granted sovereignty over the demilitarized zones. Thus, it could carry civilian work in these areas if it wished to. The only limitation, according to Israel's understanding of the arrangement, was the prohibition to deploy military forces therein.

Syria, on its part, vigorously rejected this Israeli interpretation. It claimed that the land was supposed to remain uncontrolled by either side until a permanent settlement was reached. Therefore, it argued, any Israeli presence in these areas, even civilian, was illegal. These contradictory readings of the border arrangement were often the main cause for shooting incidents along the Israeli–Syrian border.

Under these circumstances it was clear to both parties that there was no room for compromise, and that the dispute would come to a resolution in a power struggle. Each side was concerned that a demonstration of weakness would encourage the other country to undertake an even more aggressive policy. It is important to note that, in this period, land settlement and agriculture were sacrosanct facets of Israel's Zionist ideology. This ideology, which has long since vanished, demanded a stubborn uncompromising struggle for every clump of earth and grain of sand in the country.

Diverting the Sources of the Jordan River

Israel and Syria were also divided over the issue of Israel's National Water Carrier (NWC). This was a grandiose plan to carry water from the Sea of Galilee to the Negev, Israel's vast desert region in the south. The Arab states vigorously opposed the plan, claiming that its implementation would decrease the quantity of water which they felt entitled to receive. They were also concerned about Israel's plans to develop the Negev desert. Such a development, they knew, would bring an end to their aspirations of gaining control over the Negev or at least parts of it. Syria therefore decided to divert the sources of the Jordan River, from which Israel intended to pump water to the NWC.

According to Israeli hydrologists, the Arabs' water diversion plan would draw off 200 million cubic meters of water – two-thirds of the flow intended for the NWC. This, Israel claimed, would add appreciably to the Sea of Galilee's salinity, and would seriously impair the whole project.

Israel's position on this issue needs to be examined in a much wider context than the technological-agricultural project of settling the Negev. In the temper of the period, during which Prime Minister Ben-Gurion was the chief architect, the NWC was perceived as a vital national issue. Interference with this project was considered a threat to Israel's survival. The water carrier gave tangible expression to Israel's intentions to develop the Negev – congruent with Ben-Gurion's dream since the founding of the state. Any setback in the project of NWC would deal a harsh blow to this national enterprise and severely incapacitate Israel's deterrent capability.[1]

The Arab chiefs-of-staff met in Cairo in December 1963 to discuss the Arabs' responses to the NWC. Syria, as could be expected, adopted the most militant position. It demanded that the delegates decide on a general war against Israel, a proposal which Egyptian President Gamal Abdul Nasser strategically dismissed. He reiterated the position he held since the Sinai Campaign (October-November 1956) that the Arab states must not challenge Israel on the battlefield until they were fully prepared for such a confrontation. Syria was in no position to challenge the Egyptian stance.

Nasser was at the pinnacle of his influence in the Arab world during this period. He was highly venerated within Arab nations, and his position in the international arena was also on the upswing. He was justifiably regarded as one of the outstanding leaders of the non-aligned nations. Together with the Yugoslavian leader, Marshal Joseph Tito, and the Prime Minister of India, Jawaharlal Nehru, he succeeded in transforming the Non-Aligned Movement into a very influential organization in the international system. Nasser also scored high points in his relations with the superpowers. He judiciously and cleverly maneuvered between East and West, and was soon enthusiastically courted by both the United States and the Soviet Union.

Given Nasser's dominant stature in the Arab world and immense prestige in the international arena, his positions on all aspects of the Arab–Israeli conflict were accepted by the vast majority of Arab states. Thus, the Arab summit meeting (January 13–16, 1964) that convened on his initiative ratified his 'moderate' proposals for dealing with the Arab–Israeli conflict in general, and the diversion of the Jordan River's sources in particular. In the second Arab League summit conference (Alexandria, September 1964) it was decided to speed up the implementation of the Arab water diversion plan.

The Arabs seemed to have determined that these limited acts would be seen by the Israelis as a severe provocation. However, they believed that their relatively limited scope and magnitude would not give Israel the justification it needed to launch a major confrontation against the Arabs. By the end of 1964 the Syrians began diversion operations in areas to the north and south of the Banias.[2]

In January 1965 the Palestinian Fatah movement started a campaign of violence against Israel. The Syrians had decided to adopt the 'Fatah' organization and employ it against Israel, *inter alia*, according to the strategy of a 'people's liberation war'. This strategy was based on the awareness of Arab leaders that the current balance of forces between Israel and the Arab world precluded the option of a quick battle using regular forces in a war against Israel. They knew that in such a war they would definitely be defeated by Israel. Such an all-out war would reveal Israel's military-technological superiority, and the Arab states would suffer a trouncing.

The Syrians concluded that the Arabs must employ a different means of struggle against the "Zionist entity". "Palestine", they concluded, "must be restored by means of a long-term war – [that might take] five, ten, or even twenty years". Such drawn-out warfare, they estimated, would be painful for the Israelis; they would suffer casualties on a daily basis. Advantageously, it would demonstrate to the Arab people and the international community as a whole that the situation of war between Israel and the Arab world had not ended. On the other hand, its limited nature would not give Israel a pretext for a major confrontation with the Arab world.[3]

Israel explicitly informed the Syrian leadership – via Washington and the UN authorities – that it would not permit Syrian provocations to continue without retribution. Since the 1956 Sinai Campaign, when Israel demonstrated its military superiority against all the Arab states, especially against Egypt, it had gained a formidable degree of self-confidence. The grave fears it had before the Sinai War of 1956 from a confrontation with the Arab states had almost dissipated. Now, there was a solid certainty in Israel regarding its military superiority over the Arab world. There was no reason for Israel to refrain from a forceful response to the Arab provocations.

Furthermore, domestic criticism in Israel over the government's retaliation policy, which was apparent before the Sinai War, had subsided. The main domestic opponent of Israel's retaliation policy in the 1950s, Foreign Minister Moshe Sharett, had exited the political stage for all practical purposes a few years back. There was no significant player in the Israeli political system who could challenge Ben-Gurion's security policy. The media and public opinion had mobilized their support for the government's hard-line security policy.

Even foreign criticism had abated. The Great Powers seemed to have come to the conclusion that no threat or pressure would lead Israel to refrain from employing its right for self-defense. Israel's leadership, which had weathered heavy political pressure during the fifties, had little trouble standing up to the mild criticism of the sixties. Under these circumstances Israel was left with no reason to give the relatively weak Syrian regime any kind of break or leniency.

Syria and the Concept of the "People's War"

On February 23, 1966, Syria was shaken by a revolution. The radical wing of the Ba'th party, headed by Salah Jedid, seized control of the state. A few days later a provisional government was set up, headed by Nur al-Din Atasi, with Yusuf Za'in as Prime Minister. Initially, the American administration was unaware of the nature of the new regime and the extent of its political persuasion. Therefore, it was hesitant as to the policy to be adopted toward the new regime. The regime's anti-Western policies soon became clear from Atasi's bellicose declarations and frequent use of "revolutionary" slogans such as Syria's obligation to "struggle against imperialism", "colonialism's perfidy", and so forth.

During this time, the United States was entangled in its own conflict in Vietnam while trying to contain opposition movements on the domestic front. It therefore did not focus its attention on a comparatively minor event (as it seemed then) such as regime change in Syria. Moreover, the White House, and especially the State Department, estimated that the new regime enjoyed "popular" support and would soon solidify its position in the country.

Based on this assessment, Washington decided that it would be best not to develop hostile policies towards the new regime. The probability that any activity against the new regime would bring about its downfall seemed very low. At the same time, American leaders may have hoped that the display of good will toward the Syrian leaders would have a moderating effect on Damascus's attitude toward the West in general, and the United States in particular.

The US administration went even further in protecting the survival of the new Syrian regime: when it learned that Jordan was planning a military intervention in Syria to prevent the Ba'th regime from establishing its position, the administration exerted heavy pressure on Jordan to retract its steps. Gradually, Washington's hopes for Syrian moderation and pro-Western alignment proved to be illusory. The new regime showed itself to be overtly pro-Soviet, and acted vigorously to strengthen its ties with the Soviet Union and the radical states in the Arab world headed by Egypt, Algeria, and Yemen.[4]

As part of it's "people's guerilla war", Syria began to intensify hostile activity against Israel. The Syrian leaders had a blind faith in the efficacy of this path and in the extent of the defender's ability to counter it. The regime in Damascus made an all-out effort to expand the territorial base of its operations by launching strikes from inside Jordan and Lebanon. The Syrians must have assumed that this tactic would place Israel in an agonizing dilemma: on the one hand, it would be hard pressed to refrain from undertaking an action against these countries because of their strong pro-Western orientations, their abstention from joining with Syria in hostile acts against Israel, and their own military efforts to counter the hostile activity emanating from their territory. On the other hand, Israel would find it difficult to justify retaliation on Syrian territory when the activity being perpetrated against it was not coming from Syria, but from other Arab states.[5]

On more than one occasion Syria's tactics proved successful. In response to hostile activity originating from the Jordanian border, Israel, after much deliberation, ordered the IDF to attack targets in Jordan. But this "Jordanian focus" was not only misplaced from the start, but overall ineffective. Israel knew – and publicly admitted – that the terrorist activity from Jordan was being directed by Syria. Retaliation against Jordan only created the impression that Israel had been deterred from dealing with the "strong party", and instead had wielded its might "against the weaker one". Rather than striking at "the head of the viper" it had preferred to smite the wagging tail.

The inevitable results of this misguided policy soon followed: a sharp decline in Israel's deterrent capability, an increase in border incidents, and a reversal in relations with the American administration that was trying to safeguard the stability of King Hussein, with whom it was engaged in an intense dialogue. All these negative implications were apparent, following the Samu raid, which will be examined later.

Hussein sought to negate Israel's justifications for taking action against Jordan; namely its wish to bring about an end to the terror acts being carried out against Israel from Jordan. He explained to the American administration that he was doing everything in his power to thwart the terrorists from attacking Israel from bases in his country. His claims usually received an attentive ear, as he was one of the closest US allies in the Middle East. However, US officials were not entirely convinced of the sincerity of the king's statements.

The documentation at hand reveals that American political analysts were convinced that Jordan's security services were capable of acting much more determinedly in rooting out the terrorist activity on their soil. This assessment, however, was not exposed to the Israeli officials in US–Israeli dialogue. US officials preferred to tell the Israelis that the king was undertaking all necessary measures to at least reduce the scope of terror against Israel. These measures, they argued, would not become effective in the short run. It would take time, and Israel must be patient.[6]

In his intensive efforts to bolster his image as a leader who sought peaceful relations with Israel, the king also stated that Jordan would refrain from responding to "Israel's aggression against Jordan". The king stressed that he would adopt this restrained policy notwithstanding the intensive pressure being exerted on the government to retaliate. At the same time, the king let it be known that he could not hold back his army for much longer. This was an indirect threat targeting both Israel and the United States. It may be assumed that both Israeli and US officials were sufficiently realistic to recognize that Jordan's restrained policy stemmed mainly from its awareness of Israel's military superiority vis-à-vis Jordan, and its fear from Israel's vigorous reaction.[7]

Apart from the military field, Israel moved against Syria on the political-informational level. In this regard Israel wanted to show that the Ba'th regime had a deviant nature, even by the standards of the Arab regimes inimical to Israel. Middle East experts in Israel believed that the aversion held by most Arab regimes toward Israel was primarily for domestic or inter-Arab purposes. Reflecting hostility towards Israel, they believed, would preserve, and may even enhance the stature of their regimes within their own nation and the whole Arab world. Syria's case, however, was different. Its ideological world view was based on the unremitting effort to upset the status quo in the Middle East. Its leaders believed that only the absolute destruction of the existing order by means of a "people's war" would enable the building of a new world order that was better (for the Arabs) than the previous one.

It should be recalled that in the mid-sixties the international system viewed the concept of a "people's war" as though it was surrounded by a mythological aura. This was largely due to the impressive guerilla victories in Algeria (against France), South America (against existing pro-American regimes), and Vietnam (against the United States). These movements managed to convince large portions of international public opinion that they were fighting for the realization of a just cause against corrupt regimes. The strong likelihood that similar success would spread to the Middle East undoubtedly added to the unwillingness of the West to oppose the Syrian regime. To many it seemed unwise to stand against an inevitable reality. Under these circumstances it was only natural that Israel's apprehensions about the Syrian regime reached unprecedented levels.

Given these circumstances, many Israelis were gradually drawn to the conclusion that the "Syrian problem" would not be resolved by conventional military responses such as those activated in the framework of the retaliation policy of the 1950s. That policy had been designed to force the Arab regimes to halt hostile activity against Israel from their territory. If they refused, Israel threatened they would continue to feel the wrath of Israel's punitive acts.

This policy, it was claimed, was unsuited for the struggle against the new militant regime in Damascus. The past rules of the game had changed and were no longer valid. The Ba'th regime adopted an extremely militant and radical policy towards Israel. This destructive policy compelled Syria to persist in violent activity against Israel, even if the price it had to pay was high and by any rational criteria – going against its own national interests. Therefore, regular military responses – similar to those which had been undertaken by Israel in the 1950s – would not be appropriate for the present case. Now, Israel's responses had to be aimed at the eradication of the current regime in Syria. This was deemed to be the only way to terminate Syria's hostile activity.[8]

The Egyptian–Syrian Defense Pact

The heightening of tensions in Israeli–Syrian relations raised the assessment that the Syrian leadership was heading toward a full-scale confrontation, despite Damascus's awareness of its military inferiority vis-à-vis Israel. In pan-Arab forums Syria claimed that its anti-Israeli activity was being carried out for the benefit and support of the entire Arab world. Syria's leaders claimed that Syria alone, of all the Arab states, was sincerely committed to proving to the world that the war against Israel still prevailed regardless of the signing of Armistice Agreements. For this reason Syria believed that Egypt, as leader of the Arab world, should grant it security pledges in the event that border clashes spiraled out of control and led to an all-out war with Israel.

Egypt's leaders hesitated as to whether Egypt should accept Syria's appeals for a defense pact. Egypt realized the risks: if Israel attacked Syria, despite Egypt's pledge to come to Syria's aid, then Egypt would be faced with an excruciating choice. If they were to respond with military action, Israel would be justified in counterattacking Egypt, at a time when Egypt had admitted that it was unprepared to repel such an attack. Alternatively, if Egypt abstained from coming to Syria's assistance, its status and credibility in the inter-Arab arena would be seriously damaged. It would be perceived as a paper tiger, a nation that pretended to be the leader of the Arab world but in reality was incapable of defending its "Arabs brothers" against the "Zionist state".

Notwithstanding those considerations, Egypt eventually decided to accept Syria's appeals for a defense pact. The need to preserve its status as the leading nation of the Arab world left Egypt with no practical alternative. However, it seemed that Egypt's reasons for agreeing to the security pledges were directly opposite to those of Syria. They may have figured that such a pact would deter Israel from escalating the border incidents into a full-scale war, in which Egypt had no interest whatsoever. By the same token, Egypt may have hoped to obtain greater influence in restraining Syria, bringing its uncontrolled drive towards an all-out confrontation with Israel to a halt.

A high-level Syrian delegation arrived in Egypt on November 1, 1966. After several days of discussions the two states signed a defense agreement that affirmed the following points: any armed attack against either of the states would be considered as aggression against both of them. The agreement also guaranteed that in case of war, the Egyptian Chief-of-Staff would take command of both countries' armies.

Syria rightly viewed the defense pact as an achievement on its part. The pact expressed Egypt's unqualified recognition of the Ba'th regime, which had been officially installed in power only a few months earlier. The agreement also reaffirmed Syria's belligerent strategy toward Israel. From the Syrian perspective, Israel's frequent retaliation against Jordan, rather than Syria, was proof of the deterrent dimension inherent in the agreement.

The Ba'th leaders rightly acknowledged that Israel was fully aware, and had even made public statements to the effect, that the source of the hostile activity being launched from Jordan was, in fact, Syria. Despite this, Israel refrained from penalizing Syria. Rather, it preferred to punish a state that was considered a close ally of the West and that was struggling to restrict the flow of terrorism into Israel. Syria concluded, with much justification, that Israel's reluctance to allow events to ascend into a major conflict was because of its fears that Egypt – committed by its bilateral defense pact with Syria – would join the fighting alongside Syria.[9]

The Syrian thinking clearly reflects the validity of the principle that retaliation tends to bring about escalation, and eventually an all-out confrontation. However, the same could be said with regard to a lack of retaliation or even limited and restrained retaliation in the face of provocations. Such a policy tends to encourage the provocative state to escalate its provocations against the other state, as it will always be tempted to test the others' patience. Step by step it will almost certainly raise the scope and severity of its provocation, until eventually the other side will have to respond to a greater degree. From this point the probability of an all-out war is greatly heightened. Indeed, this was the sequence of events which led to the Second Lebanon War (July–August 2006) and the Cast Lead operation in Gaza (December 2009).

The Strategic Nature of the Syrian Threat

With the deterioration in Israeli–Syrian relations many circles within Israel's defense establishment, especially the IDF, came to the conclusion that the answer to the Syrian challenge would have to be "thorough and radical". The sporadic responses that characterized retaliatory operations in the 1950s, they stressed, would not curb the hostile activity that was being aided and abetted by the Ba'th regime. A limited Israeli action, it was estimated, would fail to provide a basic long-term solution and probably not even bring about a short-term lull. Summing up, the solution to the "Syrian problem" would have to include the removal of the current regime. Supporters of this policy rightly claimed that such an outcome would basically serve the United States' interest. Notwithstanding public condemnation of the Israeli "aggressive moves" against Syria, it was reasoned that the United States would highly welcome such an outcome.

These lines of thinking appear to have been the backdrop to Israel's escalation policy toward Syria prior to the Six Day War. As far as can be determined, the policy was designed to push the Syrian regime into a corner, where Syria would suffer the consequences of severe Israeli reprisals. It would, most probably, avoid a decisive counter-response because of Syria's fear from wider Israeli retaliation. This behavior would demonstrate the regime's awareness of Syria's inferiority vis-à-vis Israel. The assumption was that at a certain stage the havoc being wreaked upon Syria by Israeli military action would become intolerable. At this point the Syrian regime would have to reassess its policies towards the Jewish state.

In the framework of this assessment, Syria would most likely realize that the price entailed in pursuing its hostile policy was much costlier than the benefits it would gain. Once the regime had "seen the light", Israeli thinking assumed, it would cease its provocative behavior or at least drastically curtail it. If, on the other hand, Damascus decided to intensify its responses in proportion to Israeli retaliations, then at some stage the circumstances would warrant a quick and massive Israeli strike. Such a move would probably undermine, or at least enervate and demoralize, the current regime in Syria. In any case, Israel was going to be the winner.[10]

Israel's escalation policy that went into effect in between 1966 and 1967 was in many respects a fitting answer to the magnitude of the Syrian threat. A number of studies dealing with the Syrian threat during that period of time have generally presented it as a limited phenomenon, which should be examined in the framework of two parameters: (a) terrorist activity stemming from Syrian territory and other Arab states, and (b) diversion of the sources of the Jordan River. However, this approach seems to depict the Syrian threat in a dimension too narrow and limited to justify Israel's escalation policy.

The Syrian threat was much more wide-ranging than initially perceived. It wished to accomplish a far-reaching strategic goal – undermining the status quo in the Middle East that had been created after the Sinai Campaign, which Israel had a vital interest in preserving. In order to establish the truth of this viewpoint it is necessary to return to the Sinai Campaign and examine its results.

At the conclusion of the Sinai Campaign a new status quo was created in the Middle East – an arrangement completely different from the previous one. Israel found itself in possession of several significant advantages: (a) Its deterrent power vis-à-vis the Arab world in general, and Egypt – in particular, was strengthened, (b) hostile activity against Israel, in particular from Gaza, was sharply reduced, especially in daily security matters, (c) Israel's political stature was enhanced, (d) the superpowers ceased initiating plans for an Arab–Israeli arrangement that included Israel's withdrawal from the armistice lines and return of the 1948 refugees, (e) the status of Jerusalem, a divided city, as Israel's capital was no longer significantly questioned, (f) Israel could afford itself to channel growing resources to socio-economic needs, (g) Israel had concluded an informal strategic alliance with various states on the periphery of the Middle East: Iran, Turkey, Morocco, and Ethiopia; and (h) Israel began to develop a nuclear option that would dramatically alter its strategic position.

With all these advantages as the fruits of victory, Israel's desire to preserve the post-1956 war status quo became clear. Never before had Israel been in a better situation, its political position stronger than ever. Economically Israel enjoyed unprecedented prosperity (that continued until the recession of the mid-1960s). On the security level, relative calm prevailed. Conventional wisdom held that an Arab attack in the foreseeable future was extremely unlikely, especially in light of the decline in daily security tension. Who could ask for more?

This was the state of affairs by whose standard we have to examine the dangers that Syria's hostile activity presented to Israel prior to the Six Day War. The Syrian menace was not limited to daily security matters and Israel's water sources; it was a far-reaching strategic threat to the region's status quo. The perpetuation of this status quo was in Israel's chief interest because of the aforementioned advantages. In addition, most of the states in the region, and the superpowers, were keenly interested in safeguarding the status quo. Therefore, it is necessary to analyze Israel's responses to Syria, and especially Israel's escalation policy, in light of the dimensions and implications of the Syrian threat, which had just been described.

2

Israel and the Hashemite Kingdom
Formulation of the Tacit
Israeli–Jordanian Strategic Alliance

The Jordanian regime under King Hussein's leadership strived to maintain the status quo with Israel. The convenient standards for this relationship had been set down after the War of 1948, based chiefly on the secret and informal strategic understanding reached during the war. At the heart of this mutual understanding, sometimes referred to as "collusion", was the awareness of the leaders of both states that the Palestinian national movement was a threat to both countries. Therefore, Israel and Jordan shared a common interest in preventing the Palestinians from realizing their goal of self-determination in the territory of either country.[1]

In practical terms both states realized that beyond their manifold disputes, they shared a common *raison d'être* – preservation of their unique political identity – that made it incumbent on them to establish a broad strategic understanding. A major element in this understanding was that only two states could exist between the Jordan River and the Mediterranean Sea – Israel and Jordan. This meant that both states would reject the establishment of a third, Palestinian state, between them. However, since this arrangement did not include a mutually accepted boundary line, disagreements and even military clashes were liable to emerge.

But these "unfortunate misunderstandings" could not detract from the wider strategic perception based on the common threat both states faced. Israel and Jordan preferred not to enshrine these understandings in written documents, believing this would not serve their best interests for the following main reasons:

1. Such an understanding stood against the essence of the United Nations Resolution on partition. This resolution, adopted by the General Assembly on November 29, 1947,

envisaged the establishment of an Arab (Palestinian) state and a Jewish state.

2. Jordan would be extremely embarrassed if it was known that it had been collaborating with the Zionists against her "Arab brothers". Consequently, her position in the Arab world would be severely jeopardized.

3. Both parties knew there was no need for such a formal document: the quest for survival of both states was stronger than the clause or subsection of a formally signed paper.

Implementing these understandings proved to be another matter. The Hashemite kingdom faced serious challenges in maintaining the status quo with Israel. The obstacles came from two directions: other Arab states – especially Egypt and Syria – and domestic opposition. The vast majority of Arab countries rejected Jordan's demand to be considered the representative of the Palestinian people. On April 24, 1950, Jordan announced its decision to annex the West Bank to her territory, a decision the Arab world responded to with a refusal to acknowledge Jordanian sovereignty in this area.

On the home front the monarchy faced more drastic problems. The vast majority of Jordan's population were Palestinians who did not regard the Hashemite regime or its leader, King Hussein, as representative of their needs and aspirations. President Nasser's meteoric rise in the Arab world strengthened the Arabs' militant-revolutionary wing and intensified domestic and external pressure on moderate, pro-Western Arab regimes – especially Jordan. Under these circumstances, Jordan's stability occasionally seemed to be on the verge of collapse.

In 1955, when the Jordanian government opted to join the Baghdad pact (a pro-Western alliance designed to block Nasser's bid for leadership of the Arab world) together with Britain, Turkey and Iraq, rioting broke out. Jordan's efforts to become integrated in the pact signaled the monarchy's identification with forces considered "colonialist" by many circles in the Arab world. The king's pro-Western orientation was also scorned by a large number of Jordanian citizens, whose opposition was expressed in anti-government demonstrations. The dimensions of the protests, some of them highly violent, threatened to throw normal life in the kingdom into turmoil. The king succeeded in re-establishing law and order only after taking stringent political and military measures.[2]

In the summer of 1958 riots erupted in Jordan, again imperiling the regime's stability. Hussein assessed that his forces were insufficient to reduce the size and intensity of these demonstrations, and was compelled to turn to the United States and Britain for assistance. The British government replied favorably and dispatched military units to Jordan in an airlift operation. In order to facilitate their arrival, London asked Israel to allow British transport planes to fly over its territory. Israel agreed, aware that the Hashemite regime's survival served its own vital interests too. British troops helped the king restore quiet to the kingdom, and for the next few years Jordan remained relatively calm.[3]

In 1963 Jordan witnessed another wave of violent protests. This time the people demanded, *inter alia*, that Jordan join the "Tripartite Union" (Egypt, Syria, and Iraq) that had been created in April of that year under Nasser's leadership. Again the Hashemite regime faced imminent collapse. Hussein had knowledge of Egyptian and Syrian involvement in the riots, neither country making any effort to conceal their aim to replace the Jordanian monarch with a revolutionary regime that would cooperate with them.

Similarly to 1958, the king turned to the United States and Britain for help in subduing opponents at home and abroad. This time, however, he quickly gathered that something had completely changed in the Western superpowers' attitude since 1958. The superpowers were now acting on the basis of an entirely different situation assessment. In the early 1960s the west began to regard Nasser as a rising star in the Arab world and in the international arena; in the Arab world he became known as the most admired symbol of Arab nationalism. Within the international community he earned a highly prestigious position, due, among other things, to his success in forging a bloc of non-aligned nations, whose weight in the international system was increasing during this period. This bloc was headed by Nasser of Egypt, Jawaharlal Nehru of India and marshal Tito of Yugoslavia.[4]

This was the background to the superpowers' realization that they were on a collision course with Nasser. Trying to oust him from the leadership of the Arab world would be both ineffective and self-defeating. For all practical purposes, pursuit of such a course would only strengthen his status, bringing the Western powers into an inevitable clash with the ascending "mainstream" in the Arab world. Instead of engaging in a fruitless struggle against Nasser, the Western powers concluded that they should strive to distance him from the Soviet bloc and nudge him into the Western camp. This goal was considered attainable, especially in light of Nasser's awareness that Egypt needed Western economic aid and his willingness to put the Arab–Israeli conflict on hold for the near future. This political thinking became most effective during the Kennedy administration.

Also, wide circles in the West felt that Hussein's regime was inherently unstable. They claimed that the majority of Jordan's population was Palestinian and therefore refused to view the Hashemite regime as the representative of its interests. The severe clashes that broke out between the Hashemite monarchy and Palestinians in the fifties and sixties added a festering historical memory to the inherently tense relationship between the sides. The Arab states that defined themselves as "revolutionary regimes" – first and foremost Egypt and Syria – joined the "playing field", calling publicly and secretly for the downfall of the Hashemite regime.

On the international level the Jordanian monarchy's status was faltering. Many observers in Britain and the United States regarded the king as an immature figure, a still developing, pleasure-seeking youth. He was perceived as incapable of adequately fulfilling the roles and responsibilities which were necessary to unite and rule his fractured kingdom. The king's ability to withstand the turbulence which was expected to hit Jordan from time to time was seriously doubted by many experienced observers, and his ability to establish a stable and viable status in the international community was questioned even more.

The Western powers increasingly realized that they had to adopt a more "realistic" policy towards Jordan, the basis of which would be the awareness of the folly in acting against the rising wave of Nasserite nationalism. The Western powers were convinced that this nationalist trend would eventually sweep the entire Arab world, regardless of the actions taken by Western powers and their allies in the region. If indeed Arab nationalism was the "wave of the future", they asked rhetorically, why fight it and evoke the enmity of the entire Arab people? Under these circumstances it would be wiser to accept the emerging reality, try to "flow" with it, and derive the maximum benefit from the Arab world.

The Hashemite monarchy quickly understood the practical meaning of this new and threatening policy direction. Its message was clear: the West was basically interested in the ongoing survival of the Hashemite Kingdom and King Hussein. However, it would not intervene militarily to save his regime, as it did in 1955, 1958 and 1963, essentially leaving Hussein to his own fate. If he survived by relying on indirect Western aid and loyal supporters in the kingdom – then so much the better. If he sank, however, the West would not mourn his loss.

The rationale behind adopting this policy was based on the following main arguments. The Hashemite regime was "traveling" on borrowed time: the majority of the Jordanian people were Palestinians who did not consider the Hashemite regime as one that really represented them. They were convinced that the Hashemite leadership ruled over the kingdom only because of its support from Western superpowers. However, the fact that King Hussein maintained close and intimate relations with the Western superpowers would not prevent the realization of this trend at one stage or another in the future.

Under these circumstances the West should have adopted a new policy towards Jordan and its regime. The best policy for the Western superpowers had to be based on practical "gain and loss" criteria regarding matters of national interest. Historical sentiments towards the Hashemite King and previous obligations to support Jordan in times of crisis were almost irrelevant as far as this need was concerned. Such considerations would almost certainly lead Western powers to the conclusion that they should not support the regime by military means, in case it would again be in danger.

Israel, however, had a different agenda regarding the Hashemite regime's survival. The possibility of Jordan's collapse and the emergence of a pro-Egyptian, militant nationalistic regime in its place kept the Israeli leadership, headed by David Ben-Gurion, awake at night. The Jordanian border was Israel's longest and most tortuous frontier. Israel's ability to defend it with its small army – against an all-out attack, or even maintaining daily security – was extremely limited. Furthermore, the Jordanian border ran close to Israel's population centers in the middle of the country and to Jerusalem, the capital.

The political leadership's strategic nightmare was that Arab armor and infantry units deployed on the eastern border would slash through the narrow centre of the country in a massive assault and split Israel in half. According to professional assessments, Israel's ability to counter an attack of this nature, especially if it occurred unsuspectingly, was very limited. The Israeli intelligence community enjoyed a highly prestigious status, with reliable knowledge on the Arab world in general and on Jordan in particular. Nevertheless, it was still impossible to be certain that Israel would be able to detect an attack launched by Arab states.

Under these circumstances it is clear why the existence of the Hashemite regime was perceived by Israel as being crucial for its defense. The Israeli leadership rightly estimated that as long as the Jordanian regime maintained its unequivocally pro-Western orientation, the likelihood of a massive premeditated strike against Israel along its eastern border was slim.

For many years Israel had been the target of hostile activity along the Jordanian border, perpetrated by murderous Palestinian saboteurs as well as the Jordanian army itself. Occasionally, these acts led to major confrontations between Jordan and Israel. However, it seemed that both sides always acted under virtually agreed upon "rules of the game", which both were very cautious not to ignore. The Israeli leadership on its part was always aware of the Hashemite regime's self-restraint and determination not to permit the Palestinian terrorist organizations to cross "red lines", in their operations against Israel.

To sum up we may conclude that over the years there were tacit, certainly unwritten, strategic understandings between Israel and Jordan governing their border relations. These understandings implied that the tension along the border would remain in a relatively low profile framework; that the Jordanian regime would not undertake operations which might precipitate a war, and it certainly would not initiate highly belligerent or warlike activities against Israel.

These strategic considerations formulated the background behind Israel's hard-line security doctrine that viewed the monarchy's survival as a strategic asset of the first order for Israel. Consequently, Israel made it perfectly clear to all relevant factions in both the international community and the region that it would not allow the Hashemite monarchy to be replaced by a pro-Nasser militant revolutionary regime. If this occurred, Israel made it evident that it would invade and occupy the West Bank, or at least parts of it.

The adoption of this doctrine did not imply that Israel was always satisfied with Jordan's policies. In fact, very often Israeli officials accused Jordan of initiating hostile activities against Israel along the border. Israel claimed that Jordan had been giving indirect permission to Palestinian terrorist groups to carry out violent operations against her. Occasionally Israel reminded the international community that it was highly displeased with Jordan's failure to uphold its commitment to the Armistice Agreement, condemning Jordan's refusal to allow Jews access to the holy places in the West Bank, specifically the Wailing Wall.

However, all these frictions could not jeopardize the basic belief of all Israeli leaders, both within the government and in the opposition, that the monarchy's survival was a strategic asset for the Jewish state. Against this backdrop, Israel spoke both openly and confidentially to the Western superpowers, stating that if the Jordanian monarch was overthrown it reserved the right to invade and occupy the West Bank.[5]

Jordan realized that both it and Israel faced the common enemy of Arab radicalism headed by Egypt, Syria, and the Palestinian national movement. Under these circumstances, the Hashemite leadership was convinced that having Israel as a powerful neighbor was a guarantee for the kingdom's survival. As a gesture of "gratitude" to the State of Israel for its critical role in guaranteeing Jordan's survival, King Hussein granted Israel a tacit pledge – albeit a constrained one – that Jordanian territory would not serve as a staging area for a full-scale military attack against Israel.

This doctrine, in effect, reflected Israel's formal acceptance of the territorial status quo created after the War of 1948. This status quo entailed that Jordan controlled the West Bank, which included most of the Jewish holy places, such as Jerusalem's old city, Bethlehem and Hebron. Ben-Gurion often reflected conflicting views on this status quo, at times expressing grave regrets that Israel refrained from occupying parts of the West Bank, particularly the old city of Jerusalem at the final stages of the War of 1948. He usually accused Foreign Minister Moshe Sharett that his opposition to such an operation forestalled that occupation.

At other times, however, Ben-Gurion stated that capturing the West Bank could not be perceived as a realistic option given the existing demographic and political circumstances, as such an occupation would entail the absorption of hundred of thousands of Arabs into Israel. This development, Ben-Gurion feared, would create a situation whereby Israel's democratic nature would be seriously compromised. He stressed that if Israel was unable to maintain a substantial Jewish majority over the Muslim population, it could jeopardize the state's existence as a democratic Jewish state.[6]

In April–May 1963, the downfall of the Hashemite regime appeared imminent due to mass demonstrations that verged on civil revolt. Ben-Gurion feared this would lead to the rise of a militant pro-Nasser regime in Jordan, therefore he issued unequivocal statements to the effect that Israel would not accept such an event. Israel, he threatened, would seriously consider occupying either all, or parts, of the West Bank. Similar messages were relayed to Washington, London and to the Arab leaders, most importantly Nasser.

Ben-Gurion's threats apparently worked, since the Egyptian leadership took them at face value. No one doubted that the IDF was capable of carrying out such a move on short notice. The Arab world must have known Israel's historical-religious ties to the West Bank, and that its seizure – especially the old city of Jerusalem – had been seriously proposed at the end of the War of 1948.

The Arab world certainly had no guarantee that Israel's occupation of the West Bank was intended as a "temporary" event, nor that the occupied lands would be returned to their former "owners". Arab states were undoubtedly aware of the fact that many powerful circles in Israel would oppose any attempt to return the land to Arab sovereignty. Egypt's estimate that Israel's threat was tangible most probably led it to back down from taking a more spirited action to topple the Hashemite regime.

After the ripples of the "1963 crisis" abated, the Hashemite regime undertook a critical review of recent events and began to consider its future chances of survival. The Royal House made a serious situational assessment of the new geopolitical reality and the way Jordan could preserve its independence and special character in the Arab world. The Hashemite leadership estimated that the Western superpowers recognized Jordan as a trusted Middle Eastern ally, and were therefore most likely to continue safeguarding its external and domestic security, providing economic assistance.

If the regime's stability began to teeter, however, Jordan's leaders estimated that the Western powers might determine that their direct involvement in its defense would extract too high a price by confrontation with Jordan's civilian population and other Arab states. In addition, the superpowers would probably consider the regime's enemies to be extremely powerful and determined, and that Western aid would fail to prevent the regime's collapse. If all these assumptions proved correct, there was a strong likelihood that the Western superpowers would refuse to extend military assistance to avert the regime's demise.

Under these prevailing assessments, the Jordanians must have come to the conclusion that Israel was their only reliable ally. Israel alone had a major interest in preserving the status quo with Jordan under the conditions created after the 1948 war. For its part, Israel was well aware that a revolutionary government on its eastern border would jeopardize its survival. Therefore, it could not remain indifferent to a tangible threat to the Hashemite regime and would have to defend Jordan's interests under the circumstances.

Hussein's recognition of Israel's interest in Jordan's survival must have added immensely to his decision in late 1963 to open a strategic dialogue with Israel at the highest level of state. In a series of bilateral talks the foundations were laid for long-term understandings between the two countries to strengthen and expand the status quo.

Jordanian and Israeli–Syrian Tensions

The Syrian regime and its militant policy in the inter-Arab arena and towards Israel seriously threatened Jordan's stability. Damascus was actively involved in a widespread propaganda campaign aimed at subverting the Hashemite regime. The Syrians accused the Hashemite monarchy of cooperating with the "imperialist" Western superpowers – and even the Zionists – and of disloyalty to Arab interests. Syria's bellicose policy toward Israel reinforced Damascus's claim that it stood single-handedly in the vanguard of the struggle against the Zionist interlopers, while Jordan, which professed to represent the Palestinians, refrained from activity that could secure their rights.

Syria's ambitions undoubtedly caused the Hashemite regime considerable consternation, challenging the legitimacy of Jordan's claim that it had assumed responsibility for Palestinian representation. There was a kernel of truth to Syria's accusations. Hussein's government was most uneasy with Palestinian violence against Israel in the first place, because it led to Israeli retaliations that endangered the regime's stability. Furthermore, the Palestinian violence also enabled them to amass power inside Jordan, under the veil of the struggle for the "restoration of their homeland". The Hashemite leadership feared that this power could one day be directed against the regime.

Under these circumstances, the only way the Hashemite regime could deal with Israel was by carefully structuring a plan that would appease Israel while at the same time appear to be supporting the Palestinian cause. This entailed the adoption of the following measures:

1. The regime ordered his authorities to turn a blind eye to the low-level terrorist operations against Israel. This, the king hoped, would demonstrate that Jordan was contributing its proper share to the struggle of the Palestinians for the realization of their national aspirations toward statehood. At the same time, as long as those terrorist operations assumed a low profile character, there was a good chance that Israel's response would be moderate, and therefore would not endanger the regime's stability. Consequently, this would enhance Jordan's legitimacy, and might even absolve her in the inter-Arab arena.
2. The regime also had to ensure that the Palestinian organizations inside Jordan were not going to take advantage of their host country's sympathy for their struggle against Israel. To prevent Palestinian organizations from enhancing their power inside Jordan, their abilities to destabilize the regime activities had to be limited, and their growth halted.
3. In addition, Jordan had to convince the Western superpowers to pressure Israel into avoiding unacceptable responses against Jordan.

In its efforts to convince the Western superpowers to exert pressure on Israel, Jordan presented the following main arguments: (a) Jordan had been doing everything in its power to thwart hostile acts against Israel; (b) even Israel, with its highly efficient army, could not stop the infiltration through the borders, therefore why should Jordan be expected to do so without such advantages?; and (c) Israel's retaliatory policy enhanced the hatred towards her, and proved that a moderate policy, such as had been pursued by the king, was not worthwhile. In sum, this policy only strengthened the Palestinians and weakened the regime, an outcome that suited neither Israel's nor Jordan's interests. The king's three-pronged tactic proved to be highly successful from Jordan's point of view, and for a long period of time enabled the Hashemite regime to survive turbulent periods. Until the Samu operation, Jordan had viewed the terrorists' activity against Israel and the IDF's retaliations as a "tolerable" equation. It enabled her to demonstrate "dedication" to the Arab cause, while the costs entailed were relatively low.[7]

Jordan's conduct in its war against Israel did nothing to assuage Syria's hostility toward the Hashemite regime. During this period, almost until the Six Day War, the tension between the two countries intensified. Shortly after the Ba'th revolution in Syria, Jordan estimated, apparently on the basis of close familiarity with the new Syrian leadership and information it gathered through its intelligence agencies, that Syria was becoming a radical state actor. This meant that it would demonstrate deep hostility toward its southern neighbor, Jordan.

For this reason Jordan wanted to act forcibly in 1966 to prevent the inauguration of a revolutionary regime in Syria. However, bearing in mind its total dependency on Western powers, it asked for American backing before embarking on such a move. At this stage, however, Washington had no reason to be suspicious of the new Syrian regime, with various assessment circles in the West pondering whether it was radically militant or not. Forceful American involvement, even if covert, against the Ba'th regime could tarnish the name of the United States and seriously harm its vital interests in the Arab world.[8]

When Jordan realized that the Americans would not support its power play to overthrow the Syrian regime, it sought political venues to achieve this goal. The monarchy made it clear to Washington that it was deeply concerned about the United States' ingratiating policy toward the radical regimes in the Arab world, especially towards Egypt and Syria. The king stressed that Syria was scheming, under Moscow's guidance, to upset the stability of the Hashemite regime, and that Jordan would not continue to tolerate such a state of affairs. Jordan would do everything in its power to counter this threat. Hussein announced that in preparing for a "life-or-death" struggle, Jordan would begin channeling larger resources to security needs, even if this cut into the kingdom's economic development. Jordan, he made clear, would not be satisfied with a "political solution". Israel received information that Jordan was working with a large group of Syrian exiles to topple the Syrian regime.[9]

3

The Samu Raid – Background and Outcome
Defining the Enemy

The Israeli retaliation raid (codename "Magressa": meat grinder) in the village of Samu in the West Bank, took place on November 13, 1966, in response to an act of sabotage emanating from Jordan. Two days earlier, on November 11, an IDF vehicle detonated a mine south of the Hebron Mountains, killing three soldiers and wounding six. Prior to this event there had been other attacks from across both the Jordanian and Syrian borders.

In October 1966 the Israeli government decided to lodge a complaint to the United Nations, in hope of receiving some form of political assistance which would lead the Jordanian regime to undertake a firmer policy towards the Palestinian infiltrators. Israeli Foreign Minister Abba Eban initiated this move, having consistently expressed disquiet over the IDF's militant responses to the Palestinian provocations. He preferred to stretch the political route to the limit in order to reduce hostile activity against Israel.

Eban was well aware of the bad historic experience Israel had with the United Nations, given his service for many years as Israel's ambassador to the UN. However, he argued that Israel had nothing to lose by choosing this political course, as if it failed, Israel would still have the option of adopting the military route. The international community would be convinced that Israel had exhausted every available option in order to prevent deterioration into a major confrontation in the area. Such a tactic would ensure a better international understanding of its military moves, when and if they became necessary. As far as the military option was concerned, Eban thought it should be carried out in a low-key manner so as to avoid aggravating tension in the region.

Israel's defense establishment did not reject, in principle, the use of political venues before approving of a military way forward. In this case, however, political moves seemed to have been in vain. It was clear to all concerned that the United Nations and its institutions would never lean to Israel's side; the likelihood of it deciding in Israel's favor was extremely small. Applying to the United Nations under these circumstances, it was argued, could only be seen as reflecting Israel's fears and lack of confidence. Given this prognosis, it is not clear what the Eshkol government saw in initiating a move it knew would end in failure.[1]

Indeed, after three weeks of foot-dragging and futile deliberation in the United Nations, Israel realized what should have been obvious from the start: salvation of Israel's security problems would have to be sought elsewhere, not within the United Nations. In the Security Council meeting of November 4, 1966, the Soviet Union vetoed the proposal to condemn the terrorist activity that Syria was waging against Israel, a setback that boosted domestic criticism of the Eshkol government.

The opposition to the Levi Eshkol government, headed by David Ben-Gurion, the former Prime Minister/Defense Minister, charged that the obsequious policy had been interpreted by the Arabs as a display of weakness and a fear of clashing with Syria. As a result, Israel's policy not only failed to deter the Arab states, but encouraged them to test Israel's level of patience. Against this background of mounting internal pressure, it is of no surprise that the Eshkol government abandoned all restraint in its response to the November 12 incident, and the government called in the army.[2]

The first and most important question that had to be debated by the government was the target of the retaliation; namely, who was Israel's enemy, and against whom should the retaliation be directed. There were two options: Syria or Jordan. There was no doubt that Syria supported the terrorists and encouraged them to act against Israel, therefore on principle it should have been considered the natural enemy, the one against whom Israel should target its retaliation. An opposite view was that the terrorists infiltrated into Israel from Jordanian territory, therefore from a legal and practical point of view Jordan should be held responsible.

Following a long debate, the government decided to launch the retaliation against Jordan. In the end, it was Chief-of-Staff Yitzhak Rabin who decided to target Jordan for retribution. His domineering personality and jarring reports that the Hashemite regime was not acting resolutely enough to root out, or at least significantly reduce, terrorist activity against Israel, had the desired effect on the politicians. In the background there was also a fear about Syria's possible response to an Israeli operation against her. After all Syria enjoyed an apparent topographic superiority, and many Israeli kibbutzim and villages were vulnerable to her strikes.

Rabin's authoritative survey to the cabinet, and his insistence that Jordan should be held responsible for acts of terror against Israel emanating from her territory, made a great impression upon the ministers of Israel. Comparatively, the king's claims regarding his efforts to suppress terrorist activity and his reiteration that it endangered the kingdom's stability, made but a marginal impression on Israeli decision-makers. The Israeli leaders were easily convinced of the necessity of a major punitive operation in Jordan, one that would deter the local population from co-operating with the saboteurs and compel the regime to intensify its efforts to suppress them.[3]

The green light for the operation was placed on the Sabbath in an atmosphere of urgency and haste. Bearing in mind the wide criticism on the scope of the operation, one wonders whether most of the government ministers were fully aware of the magnitude of the raid being ordered and its potential repercussions.[4]

Background to the Samu Raid

In the course of the operation it became evident that the IDF's estimate of the Jordanian response and amount of time the raid would take was incorrect. The military planners had assumed that the IDF's massive fire-power would deter the Jordanian army from putting up a defense. It was wrongly assumed that Jordanian commanders would be satisfied with a token display of resistance, while staying at an arm's length from the IDF operation. At the same time, the Jordanian authorities would be able to claim that the Jordanian army had fought heroically against a large body of "Zionist invaders". The Israelis also predicted that the IDF's presence would trigger the immediate flight of civilians, thus allowing their homes to be quickly demolished.

In reality, both estimates proved false. The Jordanian army chose to enter the fray in a highly courageous manner, despite their awareness of military inferiority, a decision that resulted in a relatively large number of casualties. It should be noted that the IDF could have inflicted even greater damage on the Jordanians, but purposely avoided doing so. Nevertheless, this show of restraint on the battlefield did little to soften criticism of the IDF raid by both the Jordanian authorities and Western powers. Other mishaps during the operation, such as the loss of a high-ranking IDF officer, also led to the plan going awry. The IDF found itself engaged in an entirely different undertaking to the one anticipated.[5]

After the raid, the charge was repeatedly made that the military level had intentionally enlarged the operation's parameters beyond those that were approved by the political level. According to this claim, the political level had approved of a limited military operation against the terrorist organizations. Despite these instructions, the military level expanded the raid into a much larger operation; the aim of which was not only to deter the local inhabitants or the Jordanian government, but primarily the Syrian regime. The latter assumed that if Israel was unafraid to leash out against a pro-Western regime when its vital interests were at risk, then it certainly would not hesitate to seek retribution against the Syrian regime which lacked any form of American protection. In this case, the grave injury inflicted on the Jordanian regime had not been accidental.

Foreign Minister Eban noted that there were, in effect, "three Samu operations": the one that was planned, the one that was actually carried out, and the one reported in the press. Whatever the truth, Chief-of-Staff Yitzhak Rabin completely denied these charges, as was expected. In an interview many years later he stated that the operation had not exceeded its planned parameters; it had been designed to deter the local inhabitants from aiding and abetting the terrorists. The raid had not been intended to harm the Jordanian regime.[6]

The Prime Minister and government ministers felt that the size of the force and dimensions of the raid had been overstepped. The IDF was not supposed to wreak needless damage to the target area, but the results proved otherwise. Because of the discrepancy between the civilian level's expectations and the end results, Rabin was immediately summoned before the government to explain what had transpired. The Chief-of-Staff most likely expected tough criticism from the politicians. However when they saw

General Rabin, who came directly from the battlefield, with his exhausted appearance and his dusty clothing, the ministers got "cold feet", so to speak. They treated him deferentially, and were most sparing in their criticism of the IDF's role. Since the raid ended successfully from a military point of view, with minimum casualties on the invading side, the Israeli public was supportive of it and the ministers were deterred from rebuking the general.[7]

Rabin revealed that on the evening of the raid he had increased the forces size, claiming this was done following approval from the political level. Naturally, he argued that he did this solely for strategic reasons: the Jordanian forces in the region had been reinforced, and he feared their engagement in the operation. It is uncertain whether Rabin actually took the trouble to inform the civilian level – especially the defense minister – that he had increased the attacking force, or whether he felt it unnecessary to "pester" him with such "minor details". Whatever the case, it seems most unlikely that his listeners were convinced; they probably suspected that he enlarged the scope of the operation on his own initiative. Nevertheless, nearly all the ministers preferred to keep silent.[8]

Generally speaking, the impression received was that within the Israeli leadership there was an increasing sense that the army had acted arbitrarily – not according to the instructions issued at the political level – and that it had erred in its assessment of the Jordanian response. Against this background, Israel's embarrassment and vacillation in its presentation of the raid soon became manifest. Initially, the government tried to depict the raid as a tremendous IDF success; most of the press in this period was "mobilized" to support the military establishment in general and the operation's image in particular.

Later, when the real dimensions of the raid became known, voices were heard justifying the heavy loss of life on the Jordanian side. The leading accusation was that Jordan had caused its own losses because of its decision to resist the attacking force. In the initial post-operation period Israeli officials refused to discuss the size of the force in the raid, leading to rumors that over four thousand troops, supported by many armored units and aircraft, had taken part in the operation. Only later did Israel reveal the true figures, but by that time it was too late to change the public image of the operation.[9]

On the same day of the operation, the government convened

and Prime Minister/Defense Minister Eshkol made a valiant effort to justify the decision to target Jordan for retribution. Ironically, even as Eshkol explained the reasons behind the government's decision, Israel's official spokesmen were in the midst of a propaganda campaign accusing Syria of overall responsibility for murderous acts against Israel. Eshkol's reasons were excessively apologetic, and it is doubtful whether even *he* believed what he was saying. He implied that the decision to target Jordan was due to a lack of proof that Syria had been directly involved in the mining incident in the Arava (the desert area between the Dead Sea and Red Sea) two days before the operation's occurrence. A strike against Syria under such circumstances, he implied, would have been considered unjustifiable.[10]

Eshkol further acknowledged that Jordanian authorities had made some effort in thwarting hostile activity against Israel, but generally its efforts were not enough to show any substantial results. According to the Prime Minister, Israeli assessment circles could not say whether Jordan's failure to curb terrorist acts launched from within its territory was due to objective constraints or its unwillingness to unleash full power against the perpetrators. Whatever the case, Eshkol tried to explain that the Israeli operation was aimed at a Jordanian village, rather than at the entire regime. The operation had chosen a specific target in order to achieve maximum deterrence in the region. He believed that an operation of this type might benefit circles in Jordan that wanted to combat the infiltrators more effectively.[11]

The daylight operation employed armor and infantry against the Jordanian village of Samu because it was suspected of being the base of the terrorists that were infiltrating Israel. Rabin stated to the United States military attaché in Israel that four hundred and twenty troops, eight centurion-type tanks, and fifty halftracks were involved in the operation. Israel suffered one casualty, eleven were wounded, sixty houses were blown up, fifteen Jordanian soldiers killed, four Jordanian civilians were killed and seventeen wounded.[12]

Government circles in Israel and abroad could not avoid wondering whether the Samu operation was carried out only with pure security considerations in the mind of the Israeli decision-makers, or if they also intended to attain internal political objectives. Prior to the operation Israel had been in the throes of a deep recession, national morale was low and emigration, mainly of youths, had reached unprecedented levels. In addition, sharp criticism was heard in many quarters of society regarding the government's functioning, especially of the role of Prime Minister/Defense Minister, Levy Eshkol.

The criticism focused on two major areas of security: first, the security agencies' failure to halt, or at least significantly reduce the level of hostile activity against Israel; second, the political level's inability to control the military. In this light, it was suggested that the Samu raid was intended to divert public attention from these problems, demonstrate the government's determination in dealing with security matters, and create a focus of identification with the government and its leader.

The Egyptian Foreign Minister, Mahmud Riad, gave unambiguous expression to this view in talks with the Canadian ambassador in Egypt. Riad noted that the Samu operation must be seen in light of Israel's severe internal political and economic situation. Given this background, the Israeli government could not have been expected to allow sabotage and murder to continue from Jordanian territory. The public had been pressuring the political system to let the army handle matters; the country's morale was at an all-time low and complaints against the government at an all-time high. The continuation of terrorist acts would have undermined the government and its leader, with far-reaching consequences at an economic and political level.[13]

The Jordanian Response

The Samu operation produced heavy shock waves throughout Jordan. Rioting erupted in the West Bank, protestors demanding that the king provide citizens with weapons for self-defense (presumably against Israel). The regime acknowledged the realization that it was in the midst of a major crisis. Weapons in the hands of civilians would have little effect on Israel; by the same token they would enable the monarchy's enemies to expand their opposition and intensify subversive acts against the regime.[14]

This time the demonstrations were marked by different reactions on the two banks: the West Bank seethed and stormed, while the East Bank remained relatively quiet. Moreover, rancor penetrated the two populations, with mass fights breaking out at Amman University between Palestinian and Jordanian students.

The regime's efforts to integrate the two banks and "Jordanize" the West Bank seemed to have been swept away in a single blow. The years that the king and his government had spent anchoring their authority over the West Bank were wiped out in the first serious test. The regime was shaken to its foundations, and the aftershocks were also felt in the Israeli government.[15]

Jordan's enemies in the Arab world – especially Egypt and Syria – exploited the turmoil by lashing out with a scathing criticism towards Hussein. They claimed that the Hashemites were struggling against forces intent on strengthening Arab nationalism – first and foremost Egypt and Syria – and cooperating with the Arabs' enemies. The Israeli raid, they claimed, proved the futility of the king's ingratiating policy, demonstrating the Jordanian regime's failure to defend the Palestinian people. If the regime was unable to protect its citizens then it should at least supply weapons to the villages adjacent to the Israeli border, and the king should allow PLO forces to be stationed in the area to "assist" in the struggle against Israel.[16]

The Hashemite regime countered this poisonous propaganda with labyrinthine, self-justifying explanations about Israel's "perfidious aggression". Jordan reproached Egypt and Syria for failing to help a neighboring Arab state when it was brutally attacked, charges that made little impression on the Arab world. Under these circumstances, King Hussein felt that his regime was in substantial danger, the only "ray of light" in the crisis being the army's staunch loyalty to the royal house. Eventually the king's zealous efforts combining tough and soft measures paid off; within a relatively short time peace was restored to the kingdom.[17]

Years later Hussein gave an interview in which he sharply criticized the Samu operation. Hussein turned down Israel's claim that Jordan had not taken real measures to curb infiltration. He recalled that the regime had not only opposed terrorist acts against Israel, but tried to intercept them. In any event, he stressed, even if Israel was justified in retaliating, it should not have targeted a Jordanian village. Granted that Israel intended to smite the terrorist organizations (as it repeatedly declared), and not the Jordanian regime, it had to understand that in practice the raid almost dealt the regime a "knockout punch".

The king seemed to have been saying that he would have suffered the Israeli operation with greater understanding and tolerance had it been directly aimed at the terror organizations in

Jordan, organizations that threatened to destabilize his regime. Despite this, Hussein's admissions fall short of answering Israel's justifications for the raid. Israel did not accuse Jordan of failing to counter terrorist activity, but for not making a substantial effort to halt it. The Jordanians may have chalked up an occasional success, but the general trend on the ground was to "turn a blind eye".[18]

The king also pointed to the imbalance between the incidents preceding the operation and the size of the raid. He may have been implying that the terrorist act that triggered Israeli retaliation was of a local nature, and the targets were military personnel. Such an act was within the standards of the Arab–Israeli "rules of the game", with nothing exceptional about it. This time, however, the IDF had exaggerated its response by targeting an indisputably civilian objective and employing unprecedented large forces, including jet fighters.[19]

The king further revealed that he felt betrayed by Israel, perhaps suggesting that in the three years prior to the raid Israeli–Jordanian relations had been handled at the highest diplomatic level. The two countries had common strategic interests, and formulated long-term understandings in the course of their discussions. Based on this relationship, the king believed that Israel had been strategically committed to guaranteeing the regime's stability, despite inherent differences and irrespective of the ongoing "guerrilla struggle" between Israel and the Palestinians. Following the operation's "devastating effects" on his regime, Hussein was at a loss to fathom Israel's motive for deviating so blatantly from the *modus vivendi*.[20]

Beyond the dimensions and nature of the raid, the king also denounced its timing. Israel had chosen the worst possible day to attack the village, the king's birthday. While Hussein celebrated this affair with distinguished guests – including the King of Pakistan – Israeli troops were blowing up houses in Samu. The insult and anguish to the king were immeasurable, and he could only assume that the highly capable Israeli intelligence was aware of the significance of that date.[21]

Hussein drew the conclusion that the operation was designed not only to attain strategic-military goals, but also to smite him personally by public embarrassment. The great prestige that Israel's intelligence services had won in the international system probably stopped the king from admitting the obvious reason for the raid's hapless timing: an oversight on the part of Israeli authorities' responsible for drawing up an intelligent estimate before the raid.[22]

At the heart of Hussein's criticism of Israel probably lay his concern for the future. He must have feared that the Samu operation was only a primary stage in Israel's greater plan to capture sections of Judea and Samaria – perhaps the entire West Bank. Hussein voiced this apprehension in talks with Western leaders. He was undoubtedly aware of the strident debates in Israel during the War of 1948 over the possibility of seizing territories in the West Bank, an option Ben-Gurion considered realistic. By his own account he even presented the government with a detailed proposal for grabbing parts of the West Bank, but the government vetoed it by one single vote.

After the war, Ben-Gurion declared that the government's refusal to capture parts of Judea would be a "lamentation for generations". He avoided stating specifically which areas he had been referring to, but it's probable that he meant the land between Jerusalem, Bethlehem, and Hebron. He accused his Foreign Minister Moshe Sharett of casting the nay vote in this historical decision. Hussein must have been aware of these internal proceedings, and the incessant pressure from various political circles to occupy the lands that were considered the Jewish people's "ancient birthright". The king may have expressed his deep suspicion of those long-standing Israeli "yearnings" to these lands.[23]

The United States Reaction

The international community and the American administration in particular excoriated Israel for its military raid in Jordan. Even American Jewish organizations, that automatically supported the majority of Israeli moves, expressed grave reservations concerning the Israeli embassy's demand to support this operation.

From a historical perspective there is no doubt that certain aspects of the raid were rightly criticized. However, the Western superpowers and others who had reservations about this operation could provide no adequate answer to the often-asked question: what effective alternatives did Israel have considering the acts of murder and destruction carried out against her by terrorists infiltrating her borders from neighboring states? All that they could do, and indeed did, was to parrot the hackneyed claims of the 1950s regarding Israel's retaliation operations.[24]

These claims were based on the assertion that the West understood and sympathized with Israel's needs and suffering. Nevertheless, the Jewish state had to deal with this problem rationally rather than emotionally. Israel had to recognize that its retaliation policy would not solve this problem. As far as the West was concerned, only a political arrangement convincing the Arab world to reconcile itself to the Jewish state – even in a limited manner – would provide solid guarantees to ending the violence. Western superpowers realized that an Arab–Israeli political arrangement was unrealistic in the foreseeable future. Nevertheless, in practical terms it was demanding of Israel to restrain its counter-activity and respond only with low-intensity operations.[25]

Referring specifically to the Samu operation, officials in Washington claimed, in vain as King Hussein had done, that the Israeli retribution was disproportional to the attack that preceded it. Some officials went so far as to say, half-seriously half-cynically, that the terrorist activity against Israel was in many ways similar to acts of violence in any country. Therefore, it should be pursued by law enforcement agencies dealing with criminal elements in the state. In other words, police methods, not military means, should be employed.

Israel's desperate attempts to justify the raid because of internal public pressure were received with skepticism by administration representatives. The Americans denied these allegations, claiming there were no indications that public pressure had forced the government to carry out the strike in Jordan. As far as the United States was concerned, the Israeli government failed to justify the operation as a response to the "voice of the people".[26]

American officials also accused Israel of ungratefulness toward the administration, as it had received generous assistance in a wide range of areas from the United States. They further stressed that Israel's survival was greatly dependent on Washington's willingness to continue providing aid, as no other state could serve as an alternative to the United States. Israel's retaliatory operation in the village of Samu signaled the states brazen disregard of American assistance, since they should have realized that such an operation would damage the United States' vital interests in the region.

United States officials further emphasized that Israel knew perfectly well that the Jordanian regime was a close ally of the West, and that such a vengeful raid would devastate and undermine

Jordan's stability. Israel should have assessed that the attack would damage the United States' position, both with Jordan and the Middle East in general. Israel too was set back by the operation. Another after-effect of the raid was that the influence of moderate elements in Jordan was weakened, while Israel obviously had an interest in strengthening these forces.[27]

Administration officials claimed that Israel had accurate information that the Jordanians were taking serious steps to obstruct hostile activity on the border. Israel's true interest lay in assisting Jordan to pursue this activity, but the Samu operation both abused the king and strengthened radical groups in Jordan, making it difficult for Hussein to extirpate the terrorists.

People began to agree with the radicals' claim that the king's moderate policy toward Israel and close ties to the American administration had failed to protect Jordan from attacks against civilians and the army. The radical Arab states, Palestinian elements in Jordan, and the army itself pressured the king to respond militarily to the Israeli operation, pressure that the king found difficult to resist.[28]

If Israel had to retaliate in response to the act of sabotage against its military personnel, then, Washington officials pondered, why had Syria been let off the hook? Israel was perfectly aware that Syria was the main culprit, and also conscious of the fact that Syria had adopted an overt pro-Soviet orientation and a flagrantly anti-Western policy. Thus, Israeli leaders should have estimated that the United States would shed few tears if Israel struck Damascus.

Oddly, Israel preferred to target Jordan for its retribution, thus convincing most observers that Israel had been deterred from retaliating against the Syrian regime because of Soviet support. At the same time, Israel had no qualms about smiting the Hashemite regime backed by the United States. Israel's action had severely detracted from Washington's stature, impairing its credibility in the Arab world. The Arab states were liable to conclude that their security would be better served with the Soviet Union than the United States.[29] The White House's anger thickened when they realized that shortly after the fatal incident in the Arava King Hussein dispatched a message to Israel, via the American embassy in Jordan, expressing the king's regret over the loss of life caused by the land-mine. It was clear that Jordan had nothing to do with the incident. The king emphasized his intention to continue his suppression of the terrorists seeking to attack Israel.

The message reached Eshkol at nine o'clock in the morning when the Samu operation was in its final stages. Why the king chose this method of contacting Israel, when he should have determined that an Israeli retaliation was imminent, is still unclear. He most certainly knew of faster, more direct ways of getting in touch with Israel, yet he probably figured that if the American ambassador delivered the message, it would be more effective in dissuading Israel from retaliating.[30]

That same day Eshkol also requested the American administration to relay a message to Hussein. Eshkol claimed that the king's message arrived too late, after the operation had ended. By his choice of wording, Eshkol implied that, had the message arrived earlier, it might have stalled the operation. The Israeli message stated that the raid had only been launched after much deliberation, and had targeted only a specific area where the terrorists had received assistance. Israel had not intended to harm Hussein or the Hashemite kingdom. The Prime Minister further noted that the Samu operation had taken place in the wake of the Arava incident, in which three soldiers were killed and six wounded, an event that deeply shocked the country. Eshkol hinted that the operation had been carried out, *inter alia*, because of intense public pressure on the government to vindicate the loss of life, a claim already refuted by American officials.[31]

Eshkol added that Israel was aware of the king's efforts to halt terrorist activity. Nevertheless, Israeli observers had the impression that Jordan's efforts were very limited, failing to produce the deterrent effect necessary. Fearing that the king would infer that Eshkol's criticism implied a policy change toward Jordan, the Israeli Prime Minister immediately made clear that this was not the case. In other words, Israel was interested in both the Hashemite kingdom's survival and the regime's stability. Both states, Eshkol stressed, had a common interest in repelling threats from radical elements in the Arab world. Despite all this, there were limits to Israel's self-restraint. Israel had done everything in its power to keep the number of casualties to a minimum. Eshkol concluded by expressing his hope that the operation would deter local inhabitants from abetting infiltrators. If so, the common interests of both countries would benefit.[32]

American anger at Israel knew no respite. In an extraordinary step in relations between two friendly countries, Washington refused to deliver the Prime Minister's message to the king.

According to a State Department memo, the American administration was prepared to serve as an intermediary in establishing peaceful relations between the two countries, but was not prepared to serve as an intermediary merely to justify Israel's retaliation policy. Furthermore, since the United States had updated Israel on Jordan's efforts to curb terrorism, if the Israeli message was delivered by an American official Jordan might interpret this as an expression of American acquiescence to the Samu operation. If this happened, administration representatives presumed that the credibility of American commitment to restrain the disputants in the Middle East conflict would be seriously impaired. Since the United States had no interest in relaying the message to Jordan, it suggested that Israel ask the commander of the United Nations forces, General Odd Bull, to perform the task.[33]

In addition, Washington weighed the possibility of freezing or detaining arms shipments to Israel that were meant to: (a) punish and discourage Israel from similar operations in the future; and (b) revive King Hussein's spirit, and send him a clear signal that the United States would not allow him to be harmed, even by a country that Washington considered a close ally and had links to powerful forces in the administration. In the end the White House abstained from taking such severe measures against Israel. The reasons behind the United States' commitment to selling weapons to Israel had broader strategic implications and were related to the critical threats Israel faced, especially from Egypt. Also, the arms sale was designed to convince Israel to accept Washington's request for an all-inclusive monitoring of the Dimona project.[34]

Under these circumstances, the United States could not chastise Israel so roughly. Instead, it had to suffice with a sharp warning that if Israel launched another Samu-type operation against Jordan, Washington would reappraise its entire military aid program to Israel. When the question arose in March 1967, the State Department recommended turning down Israel's arms request, primarily because not enough time had elapsed since the Samu operation. Therefore, the administration had to demonstrate its credibility in carrying out its threat to Israel.[35]

For these reasons, Israel realized that the criticism of its military operation had seriously eroded its position in the international system and relations with the American administration. Israel tried to refute the charges that the Samu raid had imperiled Jordan's stability, claiming that the dangers facing the Hashemite regime after the operation had been grossly exaggerated. The vast share of the Jordanian army had remained loyal to the monarchy. As long as the military could be trusted the regime had nothing to fear, since the army was the kingdoms strongest organized force. Israel maintained that most of the demonstrations took place in the West Bank – primarily in refugee camps – without spreading to the East Bank. Furthermore, the number of demonstrations had been inflated, since the media had intentionally "blown the number out of proportions".[36]

Israel's claim that the terror organizations – not King Hussein – had been the target of the operation was received with suspicion, if not grave doubt, by the American administration. Washington estimated that regardless of Israel's initial intentions, its operations planners must have realized that a large-scale action in Jordan would be devastating for the regime. Israel's assertions that the offensive would spur the Jordanians to pursue the terror organizations more aggressively – organizations whose activity was also endangering the Hashemite regime – and thus strengthen the government's position, failed to convince the Americans. Officials in Washington charged that this was a cynical and discursive line of reasoning, and that it was doubtful whether even Israel believed it. The president's advisor, Robert Komer, explained to the Israeli ambassador of the United States, Avraham Harman, that Washington's anger at Israel was not limited to circles in the administration known for their pro-Arab approach. These circles were mainly in the State Department, but also included individuals in the White House. The president, Komer noted, was "extremely upset", and wanted Israel to know that it "had to lay off Jordan".[37]

On November 21, Eshkol sent a personal message to President Johnson in an effort to convince the senior figure at the highest government level of the grounds for the operation and the need to tone down the criticism of Israel. In his message, Eshkol reviewed the hostile acts that Israel had suffered before deciding to launch the raid, trying to refute the moral edge in the administration's criticism. Eshkol was fully aware that this line of defense had been reiterated before the American administration previously, and had failed to yield any changes. Ultimately, Eshkol resorted to using America's interest in preserving his position in Israeli politics to his advantage: he claimed that the weakness of his government and the threat of excessive criticism would undermine its stability, and could lead to Ben-Gurion's return to power.[38]

Eshkol implied that both Hussein's regime and the current Eshkol-led government stood in the balance. He too was under pressure to respond decisively to military and civilian casualties, warning that if his hands were tied, his regime would be placed in jeopardy: "A government," he wrote to the president, "that cannot provide railway transportation between its two major cities, that cannot prevent acts of terrorism in the capital, that cannot guarantee its citizens the same degree of security that citizens in the neighboring states enjoy, is not worthy of the responsibility conferred upon it". The president should understand the immense difficulty of running a government when the electorate fears public transportation in their own country and sleeping at home because of the danger of being attacked by infiltrators.[39]

Parallel to this, Ambassador Harman received instructions from Jerusalem regarding measures that Israel was willing to take to compensate King Hussein and the American administration. The ambassador was asked to inform Washington that Israel was working to reduce tension with Jordan. Among other gestures, Israel would be ready to temporarily halt the military convoys to Mt. Scopus (an Israeli enclave which remained within Jordanian territory following the War of 1948). Israel's policy, the ambassador stressed, was to maintain restraint, but it would not withhold its response if a convoy to Mt. Scopus or Jerusalem came under fire. In other words, if the Jordanians retaliated in a symbolic show of strength without injuring the Israeli side, then Israel would probably let the incident pass without responding.[40]

Israel also informed the king that for the present, at least until the end of November, it would allow Jordan to move tanks into the West Bank only "for a display of force". Harman was told to make clear to the Jordanians that if they thought the reinforcement of Israeli troops would deter lower-echelon commanders from anti-government activity, then Israel would willingly beef up its presence immediately. The ambassador repeated his country's agreement to allow sixth fleet aircraft air passage across Israel on their route to Jordan, thus demonstrating American support for the monarchy. Israel also willed Washington to inform the king that he could transfer troops from the border region into the country's heartland to quell riots, without fear of Israel exploiting the situation.[41]

As could be expected, these tokens failed to cause King Hussein's anger to subside. His criticism was directed at Israel and the American administration. He claimed that for years American representatives had been assuring Jordan of Israel's commitment to the post-1948 war status quo, and that no serious political element in Israel viewed the expansion of the state's borders beyond the armistice line as a realistic option.

On the basis of this evaluation, American officials affirmed that Israel had an inherent interest in seeing a stable regime in Jordan, and would not take any steps liable to endanger this stability. Even if the idea to move against the regime was raised in Israel, the king could be certain that the United States' political leadership would prevent it from materializing into an issue. United States officials stressed that Israel fully appreciated and understood what its enormous dependency on Washington meant. One could therefore assume that it would never dream of embarking on an action that would fly in the face of its closest ally – the United States.

Hussein realized, however, that for all practical purposes these guarantees had been toothless mutterings. Israel had not been deterred from carrying out a massive military action against a civilian target in Jordan, even though it was aware that such a move was capable of shattering the stability of the Hashemite regime. With unbridled audacity Israel had even employed American Patton tanks in the operation.[42]

At the same time, the king bitterly criticized the administration's attempts to convince him that Syria, not Israel, was his real enemy. Now, after the entire network of American pledges and security guarantees had crashed, the only effective step Washington could take to retain credibility in Jordan's eyes was to supply it with advanced weapons systems that would deter Israel from repeating a similar operation. Hussein declared his resolve to acquire the necessary weapons for his army, avowing that American refusal or stalling was liable to undermine his position vis-à-vis the military establishment, an unacceptable development. If Washington were to deny these munitions, Jordan would seek other venues; considering turning to Moscow for an arms supply. It is highly doubtful that Hussein believed the Americans would swallow such a threat.[43]

Johnson tried to allay the agitation in the king's heart and his fear of Israel's machinations for the West Bank by sending him a message stating that the White House had rebuked Israel "in the strongest terms". In addition, the president guaranteed extensive assistance to Jordan in overcoming its present crisis. The message also informed the king that the United States ambassador in Jordan had reported the king's apprehensions over a possible Israeli policy change and Israel's aspirations to seize parts of the West Bank. Johnson notified the king that he appreciated the circumstances that led him to this assessment, but that the administration had good reason to believe that such a scenario would not occur. In any case, Washington had made it clear to Israel in the toughest language that if it undertook the military move "it would have the gravest consequences for American–Israel relations".[44]

In a conversation with the United States ambassador to Jordan, Hussein expressed his satisfaction with the president's letter and asked the ambassador to thank him for the message: "It is good to know," he added, perhaps with a shade of irony, "which of your friends stick with you in times of trouble". The Americans estimated that Hussein's fall would trigger an Israeli military intervention in Jordan. Such an act would create prolonged instability in the region and perhaps an all-out Arab–Israeli confrontation, a scenario that could seriously threaten the United States' vital interests in the Middle East. Against this backdrop, Hussein tried to squeeze as much foreign aid as possible out of the administration.[45]

In Amman, the king continued his efforts to gain sympathy and understanding from American representatives, in the hope that these sentiments would be translated into magnanimous aid packages. At a meeting with the American ambassador on December 11, the king applied his rhetorical skills (as well as his flair for theatrics) to cull his listener's compassion for the kingdom's "bitter fate". In the ambassador's report to the State Department he related that, "he had never seen the king in such a state of depression". It was obvious, the ambassador added, that the king had to muster all self-control to prevent his emotions gushing forth. At a later stage in the conversation Hussein burst into tears, explaining that even if the rebellion and demonstrations subsided, underground opposition to his regime was gathering momentum. Discord in the West Bank was greater than expected, the gaps between the East and West Banks destroying his dream of uniting the country.[46]

The king continued to play the part of the fallen hero. The army, he told the ambassador, had remained loyal to him, as it always had; however, its loyalty was fading. The king's proof of this is not clear; a feeling of desperation was spreading in the army, its faith in the regime was waning. He emphasized that foreign and internal enemies surrounded him. Syria was publicly demanding the Hashemites' demise and assisting the regime's enemies within the country. [47]

Finally, after this intensive softening-up campaign for the benefit of the American ambassador, Hussein came to the point. He demanded clarifications regarding the administration's willingness to provide his kingdom with aid. It angered the king that his Chief-of-Staff, General Amer Hamash, had been two weeks in Washington and administration officials had already given him the run around. The administration had to decide its position immediately to allow the king to formulate his response. Hussein believed that Washington was having difficulty supporting Jordan because of the relentless pressure it was under from Israel and its supporters in the capital. [48]

The king warned that if the United States failed to comply with his requests he had three alternatives, the first of which, though impractical, was to turn to the Eastern bloc. All his life he had struggled to transform Jordan into a modern, Western-oriented kingdom, thus putting him in perpetual conflict with the Eastern bloc. He could not deceive his soul and suddenly flirt with the East. If it became necessary for Jordan to adopt this line, he declared ruefully, someone else would have to do it. The second option was to launch a total war against his opponents. [49]

The king stressed that he was inclined to this option, regardless of its effect on his personal fate. He wondered, though, if he could force his loyal followers on a path that would ultimately lead to their demise. The third, most attractive alternative, entailed declaring the West Bank a "military zone", and inviting the Arab states and the PLO to deploy forces there. Jordan would remove the bulk of its troops, retaining only a symbolic force in the West Bank. Hussein was aware of the fact that this last option was liable to lead to a military move by Israel. But, in the present situation, he assessed that this was still the most realistic option. [50]

The Samu Raid's Influence on Israel's Retaliation Policy

In Israel, the raid also received scathing criticism. Former Prime-Minister/Defense Minister David Ben-Gurion eyed the operation as though it were booty waiting to be grabbed. For years he had

followed the disconcerting events engulfing Eshkol and his government, now witnessing a golden opportunity to lacerate Eshkol
and his flawed security policy. It was only natural for Ben-Gurion
to seize this opening for his political campaign against Eshkol. He
charged that the Samu operation had undermined King Hussein's
status and the stability of his regime, two developments that ran
counter to Israel's interests.[51]

Ben-Gurion also criticized the targeting of civilians. This completely contravened the government's decision (October 1953) to
spare civilian lives and carry out retaliations only against military
targets: "The Samu event," Ben-Gurion declared in a meeting of
the Rafi party, "is a political mistake. [Israel] had no interest in
upsetting King Hussein's position. The principle [in daily security
matters] was not to injure civilians." The former Chief-of-Staff,
Moshe Dayan, criticized the raid in milder tones, "The Samu
operation was wrong. It should have targeted the Syrians."[52]

The widespread criticism against the operation demanded a
soul-searching reappraisal of all aspects of Israeli–Jordanian relations. Israel had to address the following basic questions: how
important was the Hashemite regime's survival to Israel? Did
Israel have to redraw its boundary with Jordan, if and when the
conditions were created for doing so, by taking control of all or
part of the West Bank? A decision on these issues involved a number of considerations that often contradicted one another:

1. The yearning of wide circles in Israeli society and the political system to "liberate" areas – including the old city of
   Jerusalem – considered "Jewish ancestral lands" that were
   currently under Jordanian sovereignty. The political groups
   that supported this annexation came mainly from right-wing
   circles.
2. The fear that the overthrow of the Hashemite regime would
   usher in a radical pro-Nasser regime that would pose a
   strategic threat to Israel.
3. Israel's dilemma over retaliation against a pro-Western Arab
   regime – as in the case of Jordan – when it was found
   responsible for abetting hostile activity.
4. The chances of neutralizing the "Palestinian problem" in
   the event that an "authentic" Palestinian government
   replaced the Hashemite regime.

Israel created an inter-ministry committee to examine these

issues, and present the government with recommendations for Israeli–Jordanian relations. The committee concluded that "Israel had an abiding interest in the survival of Hussein's regime since it was preferable under the present conditions to any other regime likely to follow. Therefore, Israel had to act for the continuation of the regime's survival as long as Jordan kept to its current path." The committee proposed maintaining regular direct contact with the king in order to realize this objective, also recommending searching for ways to inform Jordan of Israel's position.

Within this framework it recommended the establishment of a "red line connection" between the states which could be utilized in emergency conditions, such as the deployment of foreign forces in the West Bank, and acts of sabotage emanating from the kingdom. Indeed, in post-Samu talks with administration officials in Washington, Foreign Minister Eban emphasized Israel's keen interest in the continuation of the Hashemite regime. Israel, he said, failed to understand why the king should think otherwise. Eban also pointed out that Israel would not be disturbed by the entry of symbolic Saudi Arabian or Iraqi contingents into Jordan, "but nothing larger than that".[53]

In retrospect, it is fair to say that the Samu operation was a strategic mistake. It harmed Israel's deterrent capability and gravely reduced its freedom of maneuverability. Before the operation, Israeli leaders frequently stressed their awareness that Syria was behind the terrorist activity, responsible for the sabotage emanating from Jordan. Syria's goal was to hurt Israel, while drawing Jordan and Israel into a major clash. On the basis of these accusations, that were voiced publicly and in diplomatic circles, an Israeli response to Syria's intrigue was in order. Israel's defense establishment should have realized that if it focused its retaliation on Jordan, then the Arab world in general – and Egypt and Syria in particular – would assume that Israel had been deterred from confronting Syria militarily. Israel had preferred to attack a relatively weak state in order to satisfy its thirst for revenge, despite admitting that it knew Syria was responsible for the deterioration in security.

After the Samu operation, Israel's eyes opened to the fact that its ability to retaliate against pro-Western Arab states like Jordan and Lebanon was extremely restricted. Israel's repeated claims that its pro-Western neighbors reneged on their commitment to suppress terror organizations on their soil, and that an Israeli retaliation was likely to spur them to a more determined pursuit of the terrorists, fell on deaf ears. Western officials were far more sympathetic to arguments of these pro-Western states that they were not responsible for the murderous acts against Israel. Although these acts emanated from their territory their source was rooted in radical elements in the Arab world, especially Syria.

They further claimed that their military systems were incapable of rooting out this activity, despite all their efforts. Even Israel, with its greater strength and experience, failed to eradicate this phenomenon. How then could the moderate and much less powerful Arab states be expected to succeed? The Western countries tended to accept these claims as valid. Thus, the Western superpowers' criticism of the Samu operation was a jolting wake-up call to the Israeli leadership regarding the limitations of power. It was now apparent that Israel's ability to move against a pro-Western Arab state was extremely limited. Under these circumstances, Israel had no alternative but to target its military activity against Syria, while making an effort to coordinate its moves with the American administration.[54]

4

Israel, Syria and the Policy of Escalation
Formulating Objectives

Following the harsh reactions to the Samu operation, Israel realized that its freedom of action against Jordan was very limited. Under these circumstances Syria remained the only hostile state that Israel could punish without becoming enmeshed in a bitter confrontation with the Western superpowers, primarily the United States. Only in the Syrian theater could Israel tangibly and consistently demonstrate its resolve not to play by the rules that the Syrians were trying to dictate, but to employ various means that incontestably evinced its military superiority – even if the means were considered extreme. The prevailing assessment in Israel's security circles was that a display of air superiority against Syria would strengthen Israel's deterrence vis-à-vis the entire Arab world, including Egypt, and reduce the danger of an Egyptian war initiative against Israel.[1]

During the general staff meeting of August 22, 1966, Chief-of-Staff Yitzhak Rabin elaborated on his theory about how to "handle" Syria. "The Syrian problem," he began, "is basically a political [one] . . . If I thought we could stop Fatah activity by using all of Israel's abilities against this organization, I wouldn't hesitate to employ it. However, the problem is not Fatah or other Palestinian organizations. The problem is Syria, and more accurately – the present Syrian regime . . . We have to think how [our operation] will get Syria to change its position with regard to Israel. Is reconciliation with Syria possible? . . . I doubt that a warmongering Syria can deal seriously [with Israel] on an agreement that would bring tranquility in our relations with them. I'm not saying that a single operation will finish Syria off . . . [but] a series of strikes would have the necessary clout to convince them to stop their provocations against us . . . It would directly contribute to a change in the Syrian position or a change in its efforts [to support] Fatah. Syria would never be able to withstand persistent heavy damage. As I see it, [we have to] bring Syria to the point where our strikes would really make it suffer, that is, by pummeling its army."[2]

Soon afterward, Rabin made a far-reaching statement regarding the objectives and nature of Israeli activity against Syria. In an interview with the army weekly *Bamachaneh* on September 12, 1966, the Chief-of-Staff broadly implied that Israel had to focus on activities against Syria in order to attain its major strategic goal – the overthrow of the current regime in Damascus: "[Israel's] response to Syrian acts – whether sabotage, diversion [of the Jordan River], or border aggression," he stressed, "has to be directed against the perpetrators of sabotage and against the government that supports [these] assaults and is itself engaged in water diversion operations, which might be harmful to Israel's interests. The goal must be to change the [Syrian] government's decisions and remove its motivation to carry out such operations against us . . . The problem with Syria is basically an outcome of the fact that it is a conflict with the regime, not with one policy or another. This may be similar to Egyptian–Israeli relations between 1955 and 1956, although I don't set great store in historical comparisons."[3]

Rabin's statements incurred a raucous response at the political level, the Prime Minister even reprimanding the Chief-of-Staff. He was accused of proposing operations designed to overthrow the present Syrian regime. To many this seemed an improper interference by Israel in the internal affairs of other states. In retrospect, I think we should examine Rabin's utterances primarily on the basis of their "legitimacy". The issue at hand was Israel's right to overthrow a regime that it perceived as endangering its existence or vital interests.

Undoubtedly, within the framework of normative behavior in the international system, Israel's efforts to topple the regime of another sovereign state were deemed unacceptable. It was considered intolerable meddling in the "internal affairs" of another country, and therefore illegitimate. However, according to Israel's rules of conduct and normative activity, as formulated by David Ben-Gurion in the first years of the state, subversion of a hostile and dangerous Arab regime was regarded as a legitimate move. The overthrow of Nasser's regime was defined as one of the chief

49

justifiable aims of the Sinai Campaign, therefore in this light it is questionable whether the critics of Rabin's statements had a fair case.[4]

Rabin was also rebuked for having overstepped his authority. Since his statements certainly did have political-strategic implications, Rabin had trespassed onto the exclusive turf of the political level, especially that of the Prime Minister/Defense Minister. According to general opinion, by expressing himself as he did, Rabin had crossed the red line dividing the political level from the military level, and for this reason he should be reprimanded.

The seriousness of his declarations was complicated by the public airing it received. If he had expressed his views in a closed security forum, it is unlikely that anyone would have taken special notice of them. The Chief-of-Staff chose a public venue, however, allowing them to appear in the official IDF publication. Rabin's course of action reflects poor judgment on the tactical level, as it remains unclear why he decided to go public. He must have known that such an exposure of his views on a most sensitive subject would attract fire and interfere, perhaps even disrupt, the realization of this vital objective. For this reason too, he should have been upbraided.[5]

Interestingly, even though Rabin was aware that his statements caused immense irritation at the political level, he repeated his positions in an interview published on the eve of Israel's Independence Day, May 14, 1967, three weeks before the Six Day War. In this way he gave bold expression to his independent status and determination to stick to his "guns" even at the price of chastisement by the politicians: "The likelihood of deteriorating to war today," Rabin said, "is higher than ever before. This derives mainly from the Syrians' attempts to drag countries disinclined to war into one. [Israel's] activity is intended to alter the Syrian government's policy towards Israel. Israel's regular course of action [as part of its daily security procedures] is not applicable to Syria."[6]

"In this case [unlike Jordan for example] the regime is an accessory to violent activities against Israel. Syria is well aware of the fact that we know her role behind the terrorist activity. Therefore it should make an effort to stop this phenomenon as soon as possible. [Our] response to Jordan and Lebanon applies only to states averse to sabotage emanating from their territory and where it continues against their wishes. Syria is a different case because the regime encourages the terrorists. Thus, the objective of our activity in Syria is different from that in Jordan and Lebanon."[7]

Again Rabin's statements caused uproar; it was more than merely criticism of his government views, it was because Rabin expressed things that ran diametrically counter to the defense minister. That he voiced his opinion for a second time after he had been reprehended showed his disdain for the political authority, particularly that of Levi Eshkol, the Prime Minister/Defense Minister. A considerable number of government members, who were far from being staunch supporters of either Eshkol or Rabin, sought to magnify the gravity of the matter in order to disconcert both sides and weaken their positions.[8]

Eshkol, who even before this had been dissatisfied with the Chief-of-Staff, was now determined to demonstrate his leadership prowess by clamping an unrealistic limitation on the Chief-of-Staff's public expressions. A leader as experienced as Eshkol should have known that a Chief-of-Staff as independently-minded as Rabin would never consent to such limitations, and that their infraction would only erode Eshkol's limited authority.[9]

While Rabin was publicly urging the need for Israel to undertake measures which would bring about the collapse of the Syrian regime, he presented his views with even greater resolve to his political superiors. He insisted that Israel clobber Syria into ceasing its hostile activity. The chances were slim, he felt, that Israel would get dragged into a "major" war since Egypt – the strongest Arab state in the region – would probably remain on the sidelines. During the Suez War of 1956 when Israel attacked Egypt at Sinai, Syria chose not to interfere, and there were good reasons to assume that Egypt would react similarly when Syria was attacked.

Rabin's message must have made a strong impression on the government ministers. Various figures in the country's leadership began to see that an Israeli strike against the Syrian regime might just remove an element of considerable destructive capacity that jeopardized the region's relative stability. Israeli leaders assumed, with a great deal of confidence, that such a military move, if carried out firmly and swiftly, would not entail Egyptian intervention. Other states in the region – Jordan, Lebanon, Iran, and Saudi Arabia – would most probably express understanding, perhaps even satisfaction, for an initiative that hastened the demise of the radical regime in Damascus.[10]

Israel's Assessment of the Egyptian Response

Another factor that undoubtedly contributed to the decision that Syria would be the target of retaliation was Israel's concern that the absence of a response would have negative implications on the Arab states – especially Egypt and Jordan – that favored the continuation of the status quo. The Israelis reckoned that the lack of a stiff military response against Syria would pressurize the Arab states that were fearful of the rising tension in the region into adopting Syria's militant line, and increasing border friction with Israel. The main argument that could convince them to pursue this path was that the threat of a powerful Israeli retaliation had greatly diminished. If the moderate Arab states were lured onto this track, then they could completely upset the existing order in the Middle East that had been in effect since the end of the 1956 Sinai Campaign.

As noted, in the period just before the Six Day War the president of Egypt and the country's leaders frequently expressed, both publicly and privately, their opposition to war with Israel in the foreseeable future. Nasser made it clear that Egypt would not be pulled into a major conflict until it was ready. Senior Egyptian officials informed the American government that Egypt had conveyed to Syria in the clearest of terms not to expect Egyptian assistance in the event of inflammation with Israel because of Syria's provocation.[11]

As a rule, during the years which preceded the Six Day War the Egyptian leaders spoke at length about the need "to keep the conflict in cold storage". Some officials went even further, mentioning the need for some kind of an arrangement with Israel. In a speech in November 1965, Nasser declared:

> We have to realize that Israel is not an easy problem, and those who demand brash action, actually offer Israel a victory. Thus, every move against Israel must be weighed seriously so that it would have the best chance for one hundred percent success. This is the only way we will achieve our goal and not have a repetition of the events of 1948. The road back to Palestine is not strewn with roses. It is soaked in blood and misery; war is not a game. If you can't guarantee victory – why put yourselves at risk?[12]

According to Shlomo Gazit (head of the Israeli Intelligence

Research Section at the time), in a statement made years later, there were good reasons supporting the assessment that Egypt would not wish to go to war against Israel in the foreseeable future. In the first place Egypt seemed to be a very weak state socially and economically. Secondly, the fact that a large part of its army was bogged down in Yemen in a bloody, ongoing civil war made it unreasonable that Egypt would wish to undertake the risk of an all-out confrontation with Israel. Finally, the Egyptian leadership was well aware of the fact that their country was in a militarily inferior position to Israel. All these reasons, and probably some others as well, strengthened the Israeli estimate that in the foreseeable future Egypt "would not be planning for a general war".[13]

The moderate Egyptian trend stood in danger because of Syria's militant policy toward Israel. It was obvious that Egypt could not remain on the sidelines for long in the face of the rising Israeli–Syrian tension. If it refused to play a role in the shooting incidents between Israel and Syria it would be labeled a paper tiger, incapable of leading the Arab world. Furthermore (and with no connection to the mounting tension with Syria), Egypt had to continuously rebuff charges hurled at it by the conservative Arab states – Jordan and Saudi Arabia – for its cowardly policy toward Israel. Egypt, it was claimed, was exploiting the presence of UN forces in Sinai as a pretext for shunning military operations against Israel.

Under these circumstances, the warning to Syria by senior Egyptian officials and Nasser himself that Egypt would not be drawn into a Syrian-provoked conflict with Israel, and that Syria should not expect Egyptian aid if a major clash with Israel erupted, became highly relevant. It was presented as further proof that Egypt could not assume the role of a leader of the Arab world, as it wished.

By late 1966 there were manifest signs of a turnaround in Egypt's laid-back attitude toward the Israeli–Syrian tension. President Nasser and Syrian Prime Minister Yusuf Za'in held talks during November 1–7, 1966. On November 4, the two states signed a defense pact stating that an attack on one party would be considered an attack on the other, and that both states were committed to coming to each other's assistance in case of an attack.

Israeli intelligence analysts emphasized the restraining clauses that Egypt introduced into the pact, in order to reduce the danger of Egypt being sucked into the vortex of Syrian provocations. For example, nowhere was a war with Israel mentioned, nor were there any references in the pact to a popular liberation war. Early on, the second operative section stated that the defense policy taken by the two sides had to be the outcome of joint consultation. This section was naturally designed to deny Syria the opportunity of trapping Egypt in a conflict against its interests. The third operative section held that even in the case of a surprise attack against one of the two signatories, further countermeasures would depend on mutual consultation and consent. In other words, Egypt was under no obligation to respond automatically to every Israeli foray into Syria. Moreover, the Syrian response to Israeli retaliation could only be undertaken with Egyptian consent.[14]

As in many other instances, the determining factor was not the small print in the pact, but Syria's overall feeling that the agreement would gain it an all-embracing Egyptian insurance policy for military involvement in a clash with Israel. The Syrians could expect that, in light of this newly forged "cohabitation" with Egypt, the Soviet Union too would join the fray if relations with Israel deteriorated. Thus, despite Egypt's "defense measures" to avoid being pushed into a collision with Israel, the Syrians probably regarded the agreement as a major political-legal layer cementing Egypt's commitment to Syria, and most likely the Soviet Union also. In this case, a full-blown shooting incident in the Syrian sector would test the Egyptian leadership's resolve, credibility, and claim of being the leader of the Arab world.[15]

The Escalation Policy – The United States' Positions

Given these political conditions, the prevailing assessment in Israel was that the Western superpowers – first and foremost the United States – would probably accept with understanding, perhaps even satisfaction, an Israeli-initiated strike against Syria. Furthermore, Israel could assume that the US would deter the Soviet Union from direct involvement in the confrontation. The Syrian regime's hawkish nature, its close ties with the Soviet Union, and its overt support of the people's war doctrine left no doubts regarding the Western superpowers' attitude toward it.

These assessments were obviously based upon the assumption that an Israeli military operation would produce a swift and decisive victory. A prolongation of the fighting bore the danger of

Soviet intervention on Syria's behalf. With the United States heavily committed to the war in Southeast Asia during this period, Washington had an obvious interest in preventing the development of a major crisis in the Middle East.

The reports from Israeli representatives in the United States reveal several levels of the American administration's responses to Israeli military activity. On the official level, administration representatives emphasized the basic position of the US, categorically rejecting Israel's retaliation strategy. The administration, Israel was informed, believed that such moves reflected mistaken political thinking that detracted from Israeli interests. These military acts recalled the 1950s when Israel made frequent and massive use of its retaliation policy. In American–Israeli talks, the administration acknowledged that it had no practical alternative to the retaliation policy except to suggest that Israel seeks a peace arrangement with its Arab neighbors. Be that as it may, all the parties realized that such an arrangement was still only a pipedream.[16] Prior to the Six Day War, American officials often explained to Israel that its regular security policy must take into consideration not only daily security matters, but also long-term political ones of common interest to both Israel and the United States. For example, Israel had to understand that its military operations strengthened militaristic elements in the Arab world and the trend toward Arab unity.

The Arab states, it was argued, interpreted Israel's actions as expressions of aggression supported by the Western superpowers against the collective Arab world. Domestic pressure increasingly forced the moderate regimes to respond to these acts. They, too, had to convince the Arab people that they also took an active part in the struggle against Israel. In any case, this situation bolstered the radical forces in the Arab world.

Simultaneously, since Arab rulers were aware of the difficulty in facing Israel single-handedly, a trend to unification was in sway. Both developments ran counter to long-term American and Israeli interests, therefore when the time came for Israel to decide on the proper response to terrorist activity, it had to rise above emotional predilections that demanded revenge and an immediate response. Israel had to proceed with aplomb on the basis of rational considerations in order to guarantee long-term benefits.[17]

However, together with these official admonitions, administration representatives voiced other sentiments regarding Israel's daily security policy. Some were oblique, others explicit. Their point was clear: the United States would probably react with understanding to a punitive strike undertaken by Israel against Syria. The main reason for that understanding was Damascus' close relationship with Washington's communist enemy. These signals probably echoed the efforts made by Israeli leaders, in both the military and political sphere, to reach an understanding, even a secret one, with the US regarding Israel's military response to Syria's provocations.

Indeed, in light of the sharp increase in border incidents during the month preceding the Six Day War, a concentrated effort was underway at the highest political and military levels to arrive at an understanding with senior figures in the American government on Israel's reaction to Syrian aggression. The understanding Israel wished to achieve with the US administration would be based on the assumption that Syria's policy, and course of action, threatened not only Israeli interests but also the vital interests of the United States and its allies in the region. Therefore, the US was expected to show at least tacit support in the event that Israel would decide to launch an attack against Syria.[18]

In early 1965 Rabin and the American ambassador to Israel met to discuss the tension with Syria. The Israeli Chief-of-Staff explained the recklessly aggressive nature of the Syrian regime, basing his claim primarily on Syria's support of terrorist acts against Israel. These acts were largely carried out from the territories of moderate and pro-Western Arab states such as Jordan and Lebanon. The aim of the Syrian regime was to tempt Israel to attack these states, thereby splitting the Western camp.[19]

Another dangerous source of friction between Israel and Syria related to Syria's project for diverting the sources of the Jordan River. Rabin stressed that from Israel's perspective the Syrian diversion project was an act of aggression that demanded a vigorous Israeli response. In trying to convince the ambassador that Israel had legitimate justification for attacking Syria, Rabin made a parallel between Syria's water diversion and Cuba's provocations with Soviet support on the eve of the October 1962 Cuban Missile Crisis. Even in the Cuban case, the issue was not a direct assault against the US, but involved activity on Cuban soil being carried out with active assistance from the Soviet Union. At first glance, the Cuban case could be seen as the legitimate action of an independent state on its own sovereign territory. Nevertheless, the

United States viewed Cuba's operations, and justifiably so, as an offensive maneuver. Israel, too, was justified in perceiving Syrian activity on its sovereign soil as an offensive maneuver that warranted Israeli retaliation. [20]

It is difficult to imagine that Rabin expected the ambassador to accept the accuracy or legitimacy of these parallels, to the extent that Israel could recognize that the administration was giving it the green light to continue, and perhaps intensify, its military activity against Syria. However, against the background of Rabin's explicit statements, even the ambassador's silence might be interpreted as acknowledging Israel's right to respond. Walt Rostow, the president's special advisor, gave unmistakable expression to this position. In a memo that he sent to President Johnson in the beginning of the waiting period, he recommended demanding that Israel exhibit restraint. With a surprising degree of candor, he added "a week earlier he would have advised the administration to turn a blind eye if Israel had attacked Syria. We have no alternative suggestion to offer Israel on how to combat terrorist activity that's growing increasingly sophisticated."[21]

In January 1967, the shooting incidents on the Syrian border began to intensify. In talks between Western diplomats and Syrian officials, the latter tried to brush off their responsibility for the hostilities against Israel, claiming that Israel had created an artificial atmosphere of surging tension on its northern border that exceeded the seriousness of the incidents themselves. The Syrians also charged that several Palestinian groups were operating in the area, and that Syria had no control over their movement. To support these claims, the Syrians pointed out that even the Western powers, with their limitless resources and vast security networks, failed to maintain law and order in their countries. As a result there were no moral grounds for them to demand that Syria uphold control and discipline in its country.[22]

At the same time, Syrian officials accused Israel of expelling over 90 percent of the Syrian farmers in the demilitarized zones and seeking to expropriate their lands. Syria, they further declared, had attempted to show maximum restraint. When it was discovered, however, that Israel persisted in its efforts to gain control of the demilitarized zones, it had no choice but to open fire. According to the Syrians' account, they had proposed feasible ideas for solving the dispute over the demilitarized zones, but Israel had rejected all of them. In their opinion, Israel's goal, *inter alia*, involved creating division and discord between Syria and the West. Syria admittedly feared an all-out Israeli attack, and with a heavy tinge of abrasiveness, criticized Jordan's decision to display restraint following the Samu raid. Syria's representatives stressed that their country was not Jordan, and would respond to every military operation that Israel launched against it.[23]

The Syrians also menacingly fingered the Western superpowers, warning that an Israeli–Syrian clash harbored dangers not only for the region but for the entire international system. The Western superpowers had to acknowledge that an Israeli–Syrian flare-up would have a disastrous impact on their status in the Arab world and on their economic-strategic interests in the region. It was in this context that the Syrian representatives tried to emphasize that Egypt's moderate position vis-à-vis Syria's exchanges of fire with Israel should not create the impression that Egypt had reneged on its commitments to the defense pact. It would be a grave mistake if anyone doubted, in the event of continued Israeli aggressions against Syria, that Egypt would fail to call up its military forces to the defense of Syria.[24]

Given the direction the wind was blowing in the United States administration – awareness of Israel's need to react with force to Syria's relentless provocation – the Prime Minister made an effort to upgrade and cement the understandings with the American administration. After the widespread shooting incidents throughout the length of the Israeli–Syrian border in January 1967, Eshkol relayed an oral message to Johnson in which he made a complete volte-face regarding Israel's position on the Samu raid and its justification and degree of wisdom. Instead of trying to explain the act discursively and unconvincingly as in the past, Eshkol chose a bolder, more realistic tack, effectively admitting that the raid had been a mistake, and stating that Israel had no intention of repeating "its misjudgment of November 1966".[25]

He implied that this time it intended to exert its right for self-defense, giving Syria a thorough flogging and warning of the dire consequences it would incur if provocations continued. The United States expressed no opposition regarding this position, instructing its ambassadors in Syria and Egypt to inform the leaders of these countries that Israel's patience was wearing thin as a result of the persistent terrorist attacks. Washington also made it clear that the Syrian and Egyptian governments should not look to the United States to hold Israel at bay.[26]

Eshkol's caveats, however, failed to deter Syria. Several days later, against the backdrop of continued hostilities against Israel, Eshkol sent a calming, moderate message to Johnson, stressing that despite Syria's intolerable provocations, the majority of which were directed against civilians, he intended to show restraint and avoid a devastating military response. In the latest incident, terrorists infiltrating from Syria had planted an antipersonnel mine in a soccer field in the Jewish agricultural settlement of Dishon, close to the Lebanese border, resulting in the death of one Israeli civilian.[27]

Israel's decision to avoid retaliating, Eshkol stressed, was rooted in the hope that Syria would understand the danger inherent in its continued provocation. When he visited northern settlements on January 10, 1967, he stated in clear straightforward language that Israel was not obliged to respond immediately every time Syria instigated a terrorist act. Israel would determine the time, method, and size of its reaction. Until now, it had sought to avoid escalating the situation, but it would no longer be able to preserve self-restraint in the face of Syria's determined aggression.[28]

Eshkol's reason for sending this message is ambiguous; he was certainly aware of the assessments that the administration were likely to support a powerful Israeli retaliatory strike against Syria. He may have feared that American approval of an Israeli combat operation would increase the pressure on him from the military level, leaving them more leeway to punish Syria by escalating the tension to the point of a full-blown confrontation. Now, when no one doubted Israel's overwhelming military superiority and American winks and nods in the direction of a green light, there was a strong likelihood that Egypt would stay out of the fracas if Israel carried out a quick and devastating attack. Despite these favorable circumstances, Eshkol seemed to have lacked the stomach to make a fateful and far-reaching decision, instead playing for time in the hope that some unforeseen development would restore peace to the area.

Washington responded coolly to Eshkol's moderate message. The administration expressed its admiration of Israel's self-restraint with regard to retaliation acts against pro-Western Arab states. At the same time Israel's impression was that the White House wished to inform Israel that it would not weep if Israel acted belligerently towards Syria. No government, the administration announced, can accept continuous assaults on its citizens. A leader as experienced as Eshkol would have instantly seen that such a self-explanatory statement would not have been issued unless the administration intended to let Israel know that it had permission to use military force against Syria.[29]

Furthermore, Eshkol would have inferred that this was as explicit as an official message from a high-ranking authority could get. Indeed, the administration was concerned by the possibility that Israel would publicly claim that it had the United States' blessing to launch an attack against Syria. For this the US administration wished to ensure that Israel would not be able to claim that it had justification to interpret Washington's signals as though it was spurring Israel on. Thus, the administration simultaneously restated its time-worn position that it hoped Israel would maintain its policy of restraint in the realization that its retaliation policy was not leading to a solution to the Arab–Israeli crisis.[30]

Simultaneously, senior Israeli figures began criticizing what they perceived as the government's kid-glove approach toward Syria, and the tendency to rely excessively upon passive defense for halting infiltration. In the critics' eyes, a more aggressive course of action would create an effective dimension of deterrence vis-à-vis the Arab world. In view of Israel's effort to acquire electronic defense devices, the military level felt that there was a trend in the political sphere to regard these gadgets as the ultimate answer to Israel's security threats. In other words, the military establishment had grave reservations with regard to the wide spread belief in the political sphere that electronic devices would drastically reduce enemy penetration, or at least neutralize Israel's need to respond forcefully to hostile activity.

Against this setting Yitzhak Rabin took it upon himself to point out the serious limitations of these measures. In a press interview at the end of his third year as Chief-of-Staff, Rabin stressed that basing Israel's layout across from Syria on defensive measures would fail to significantly reduce hostile activity, contrary to what some people in Israel believed. Israel, he stressed, had to build a deterrent factor, and the electronic defensive gear that was being touted as *the* answer would contribute little to the establishment of strong deterrence.[31]

In fact, Rabin promised it would create just the opposite. The conspicuous use of the devices would only encourage the Arab states that abetted the terrorists to continue their support and even increase it. Israel was duty-bound to make it clear to the Arab regimes that if infiltration continued, it would lead to an all-out war with dire consequences that would directly affect their survival. Rabin also emphasized that the sabotage being waged against Israel was not carried out independently, but under the guidance and encouragement of the Arab states, with Syria in the lead.[32]

In mid-February, the staff from the United States embassy in Israel, headed by Ambassador Woolworth Barbour, made a two-day tour of the northern border. The tour was designed to illustrate Israel's strategic-topographic disadvantage vis-à-vis Syria, and why Israel had to act as it did toward its foe in the north. The visit seemed to have accomplished its objective brilliantly. A detailed report of the tour by the Israeli diplomat, Shlomo Argov, combined a sober analysis with the hope that the American representatives obtained a firsthand look at the difficulties and dangers facing Israel.[33]

The report seems to say that since the Americans had been given an immediate impression of Israel's security situation, they were likely to exhibit a better understanding of Israel's military activity than in the past. Whether this was the impression of the embassy officials or not is irrelevant, but it is of great importance that a high-ranking Israeli diplomat, Ambassador Argov, who was known for his good relations with the Israeli military establishment, came to this conclusion. This conclusion was probably shared by other Israeli officials and high-ranking military personnel.[34]

In mid-March a group of US State Department officials visited Israel. At the head of the delegation were Hal Saunders, a member of the National Security Council, and Lucius Battle, who had just completed a tour of duty as American ambassador to Egypt. Among the sites of interest on their itinerary, the guests were taken for a tour of the northern border and a meeting with the Chief-of-Staff, the commander of the Northern Command, Maj. Gen. David Elazar, and other senior officers. The Israeli report of the meetings accurately reflected the current trend in the IDF high command with regard to the policy that should be adopted towards Syria, a policy centering upon the overthrow of the regime in Damascus. The diplomats' report also implied that some Israeli decision-makers believed that Washington would not react negatively to a military operation against Syria, and might even regard it as a positive development.[35]

After the visit, the guests explicitly stated that the American administration would relate with great understanding to an Israeli attack on Syria. One of the US officials was quoted as stating in rather undiplomatic terms, "the Syrians are bitches. Why the hell, didn't you crack them over the skulls when the time was ripe?" When Hal Saunders was asked to comment on this issue, he referred to the Samu raid as an operation that he considered unjustified. "Your problem," he explained, according to the Israeli report, "is Syria. Why then did you vent your rage on Jordan? We totally reject the claim that it was impossible to target Syria . . . When everyone knows that Syria is the party responsible for the terrorist acts on your borders . . . There would have been no need to explain [your motives] for a punitive operation against Syria."[36]

The report by Saunders and Battle to the State Department on their visit mentioned that both of them had received a strong impression that the IDF was eager for approval to execute a large-scale operation. IDF officers felt that the discussions in the Israeli–Syrian armistice commission were futile, and could not lead to any positive outcome for Israel. In talks that Saunders and Battle held with the Israeli Prime Minister, they got the impression that Eshkol also had a hawkish approach toward Syria. Eshkol seemed to think that the United States would eventually understand Israel's plans to punish Syria. The report also stated that the highest political level in Israel believed that the US would not interfere if Israel decided to attack, and might even extend tacit support to the operation.[37]

There were further signs in the dialogue between Washington and Jerusalem that the American administration would accept an Israeli offensive with understanding. In March 1967, in a talk between the Under Secretary of State, Eugene Rostow, and the Israeli ambassador to the United States, Avraham Harman, the latter compared Syria to Cuba, which in this period was considered exceptionally hostile toward the US. Like Rabin, the ambassador made it clear that "Syria would not be immune if it continued to support the strategy of 'popular revolution'". "No one should expect," the ambassador emphasized, "that Israel will reconcile itself to Syrian policy that has turned Syria into a kind of Cuba for Israel." According to Harman, Rostow listened quietly and only asked "if we had experienced many incidents lately".[38]

In a conversation between Ambassador Evron, Walt Rostow, and Harold Saunders, Saunders said that the main issue on the

United States' agenda is how to handle Nasser-style "radical nationalism", also acknowledging a move towards a "head-on collision course" with Nasser. Rostow boldly affirmed that the United States would do this "bluntly and more obliquely". At the same time, an effort was underway on the part of administration officials, especially members of Congress, to broker an Israeli–Jordanian understanding that would halt the growing tension between the two countries.[39]

The April 7, 1967 Incident

The following months witnessed an increase in shooting incidents along the Israeli–Syrian border, with tension peaking in early April. On the morning of April 7, an Israeli tractor trundled out to cultivate the fields in one of the demilitarized areas on the Israeli–Syrian border, opposite Kibbutz Ha'on, southeast of the Sea of Galilee. According to UN observers, this area had been in dispute for many years. This time the Syrians opened fire on the tractor, the incident rapidly escalating into tank and artillery shelling of civilian and military targets. UN forces in the region failed to establish and enforce a ceasefire, resulting in the Israeli air force being called in to bomb three Syrian artillery batteries in the area.[40]

Israeli and Syrian aircraft were soon engaged in a dogfight during which two Syrian Mig 21s were shot down, and a third Syrian Mig was later destroyed. Following this, another air battle developed over Tel Katzir, and three more Mig 21s were put out of action. Altogether six Syrian aircraft were downed that day. The Syrians claimed that they had destroyed five Israeli jets, however according to the official Israeli spokesmen all the planes had returned safely to base. Israel announced that one Israeli had been killed and another wounded in the incident. The Syrians admitted that four of their planes had been lost.[41]

Before the battle the Israeli air force had been put on high alert, a fact that strengthened the assessment of Western observers that Israel had initiated the incidents in order to goad Syria into heating up the border tension. Israel's working assumption, and certainly its most profound desire as well, was that the pressure would justify a large-scale Israeli offensive that would accomplish the strategic objectives that the Chief-of-Staff had laid out in closed and open forums. The fact that Israeli planes had chased the Syrian fighters all the way to Damascus and then buzzed the city substantiated these assessments even further. A major confrontation, at this point, appeared to be inevitable. The Syrians, however, chose to "lower their profile" and lick their wounds in hopes of staving off the expected clash.[42]

In the aftermath of the April 7 incident, the Israeli head of intelligence, Gen. Aharon Yariv, met with foreign military attachés. His language, which bordered on provocative swaggering, echoed the Israeli security level's magnified self-confidence at that period of time. The Israeli tone would soon change as it turned out that immunity is not eternal. The defense establishment's confidence that General Yariv expressed so accurately would soon be replaced by a sense of foreboding, apprehension, and uncertainty that Israel had not experienced since the War of 1948.[43]

At the meeting Yariv acknowledged that Israel had strengthened its layout on the northern border. Naturally he refrained from specifying the size of the reinforcements, and failed to mention that a large section of the air force's order of battle had been deployed close to the border. This force would be deployed in case the Syrians decided to escalate the situation, presenting Israel with a "historic opportunity" to deliver Syria a decisive blow that would engrave in its consciousness an agony of defeat it had never known.[44]

Yariv insisted that the Egyptian–Syrian defense pact was unrelated to the recent flare-ups between Israel and Syria. The Israeli assessment was that Egypt would only help its new-found ally in the event of an Israeli land invasion. Therefore, Yariv gave vent to the near-universal disparagement in the Israeli security establishment of Egypt's so-called obligations to other Arab states – starting with Syria. Egypt, Israeli officials used to say, was not a reliable ally, and was therefore required to demonstrate to the Arab states that it deserved to be considered a leader of the Arab world.[45]

When it was time for the test, however, the Egyptians preferred to ignore their commitments to their sister Arab states in favor of national self-interest, avoiding the possibility of a humiliating defeat in an all-out confrontation with Israel. It soon became clear that this situation estimate was closer to wishful thinking than Realpolitik. It will shortly be seen that after the April 7 incident, a process commenced that led to the strengthening of Egypt's forces in Sinai, performed under the rubric of defending Syria from Israeli aggression.[46]

During the briefing, Yariv also discussed the question of Israel's daily security problems, expressing his professional backing of the Chief-of-Staff's Syrian policy. According to Yariv, Syria was the key to PLO activity against Israel, and would continue to support the terrorist organization's operations as long as it perceived that this sponsorship did not come at too great a cost. The message was clear: Israel must raise the level of its strikes against Syria and focus them on Syria's decision-makers and their vital interests. This was the only course of action that might convince the Syrians to cease their support of the PLO.[47]

Yariv implied that the Palestinian organization was totally dependent upon Syria, thus if this backing were cut off the PLO would be forced to terminate its operations against Israel. The equation may have been logically sound, but it did not stand the test of reality. It expressed the prevalent view in Israel that rejected Palestinian existence in general, and the PLO, in particular, as an independent entity waging a struggle to realize what they termed as their "right of self-determination". The Israelis viewed them as the "pawns" of radical regimes in the Arab world, especially Syria. Years later, after enormous destruction and thousands of war casualties, it would become commonly agreed that this estimate, too, was merely an expression of wishful thinking.[48]

Yariv declared that the incident of April 7 had begun as a local Syrian initiative and not from an order higher up. Ten Syrians had been killed and sixteen wounded. The Israeli intelligence chief stressed that Israel was determined to continue cultivation of the fields in the "disputed areas", since there was no reason for Israel to yield on its position regarding the demilitarized zones. Militarily, Israel had definitely gained the upper hand. Syria suffered a heavy blow and had quickly turned tail, while Egypt conspicuously showed that it had no interest in realizing its commitments to Syria. Other Arab states – especially Jordan and Saudi Arabia – had openly gloated over Syria's predicament, and even the Soviet Union had steered clear of its badly stricken ally. On the other hand, the United States gave its silent blessing to Israel's actions.[49]

Under these circumstances, Israel continued to "nip at Syria's tail". Yariv did not mince his words, informing his listeners that the drubbing Syria received on April 7 had failed to convince it of Israel's determination to counter any violation of its rights in the demilitarized areas. Yariv seemed to imply that Israel not only

intended to cultivate the "contested fields", but would also consider taking additional steps to prove to Syria that it "meant
business". To back up these threats, General Yariv announced
that the Syrians were well aware that Israel had reinforced its positions on the northern border, and that it was perfectly capable of
dealing a severe punishment.

Yariv proceeded to say that Israel was satisfied with Jordan's
response to the April 7 incident. However, why he chose to expose
Jordanian conduct in this light is unclear. Although the briefing
was in a classified forum, his words would undoubtedly travel to
the Hashemite Kingdom and cause considerable consternation.
While the Jordanians, too, had an interest in seeing their northern
neighbor smitten, under no circumstances did they wish to be
accused of taking sides and collaborating with Israel against
another Arab state. If the truth of Israeli–Jordanian relations (that
saw eye to eye on the Syrian menace) was leaked, Jordan might be
forced to demonstrate solidarity with Egypt and Syria.[50]

Yariv was surprisingly candid before the foreign attachés in
revealing that Israel's policy towards Syria aimed at something
greater than simply guaranteeing Israel's rights in the demilitarized
zones. His bold statements clearly implied that Israel's goal was to
initiate a military strike every time Syria presented a convenient
opportunity. It appeared that Israel wanted to present the Ba'th
regime with the choice of either escalating the tension and running
the risk of a clash with Israel, or lowering its profile and risking
ignominy in the Arab world. Israel's reinforcement in the north
had been a direct result of this strategic trend.[51]

Nevertheless, Yariv stressed, Israel had no intention of attacking Syria with ground forces. Syria had not stood a chance against
Israel in the April 7 air skirmish, as the Syrians lacked any form of
a forward warning system and their pilots performed far below
standard. The Egyptian response had been to maintain a low profile, putting its air defense system on a state of alert, and the
commander of the air force travelling to Syria, but these were
merely token displays of solidarity, nothing more.[52]

Yariv's disclosures to the attachés must have made a strong
impression on them; his appearance and statements clearly
reflected Israel's great confidence based upon its assessment of
strategic superiority over the Arab states. Nevertheless, it is difficult to understand the political-strategic objective behind their
revelation. In our opinion, this was completely unnecessary, a

decision that reflected arrogance and an enclave tendency to humiliate your rivals. This appearance served no Israeli interest during this particularly trying hour.[53]

Chief-of-Staff Yitzhak Rabin was also carried away by the results of the April 7 aerial battle that ended in a humiliating defeat for the Syrians. At the same time, he did not believe that the loss would topple the Syrian regime, repeating that Israeli activity had to be all-inclusive, not simply a local affair, in order to succeed in overthrowing the government in Damascus. As for the actual course of action, the Chief-of-Staff was not convinced that ground forces would be needed to capture Damascus. Nevertheless, he made it clear that this course of action (ground troops) should not be completely ruled out, also stating unambiguously that he disagreed with the intelligence chief's assessment that the April 7 skirmish would amplify hostile activity against Israel. Finally, he acknowledged that he concurred with the assessment that most of the players in the region had discreetly evinced satisfaction with the clobbering Syria had received.[54]

Under these circumstances, the American response accommodated Israel's positions and policy toward Syria. In general, Washington's reactions were quite mild, while at the official level senior American figures informed Israeli representatives that the US expected Israel to display restraint. This having been said, the American admonition appears to have been merely lip-service. The United States' major concern in the fracas was to guarantee that pro-Western regimes in the region were not injured. At the same time, Israel was allowed to understand that it had a large degree of freedom to move against Syria. Indeed, in conversations between American and Israeli officials, the former emphasized Washington's interest in safeguarding the stability of the pro-Western regimes of Jordan and Lebanon. At this stage, Israel had finally internalized its need to take American interests in the region into consideration when making strategic decisions. In one meeting between the Americans and Ephraim Evron, the Israeli deputy ambassador to the United States, the question of Israeli military responses against terrorist activity was discussed. Evron made clear, most likely on the basis of instructions from above, that Israel knew Syria was behind the sabotage operations being waged against it. Thus, in the event that Israel decided to initiate a response, it would target Syria rather than Jordan or Lebanon.[55]

Syria's response following the incident reflects the great confusion in Damascus. Officially the Syrians repeated the mantra that they disclaimed any responsibility for Palestinian elements operating out of Syrian, Jordanian, or Lebanese territory, and had no control over their activity. Simultaneously, they tried to "spook" the US, in the hope that this would prod Washington into curbing Israeli retaliations. In a meeting with the United States ambassador in Syria, the Syrian Foreign Minister, Dr. Addis Daudi, pointed a threatening finger at the United States, warning that if Israel tried to invade Syria the entire Arab world would rush to Syria's aid, and a major war would break out in the Middle East. In the course of this struggle, he threatened, US interests would also suffer.[56]

Other elements in Syria blamed Israel for intentionally creating the friction along the border in order to gain control of the demilitarized zones first, before invading Syria. Whatever the case, Syrian officials emphasized that Damascus would not cooperate with Israel in curtailing terrorism. Syrian officials stressed their assessment that Israel would only risk an attack on Syria if it received American backing. Therefore, in case of an Israeli offensive, the Arab world would hold the United States accountable. It is hard to believe that the Syrians thought that such trumped up threats would influence American policy and reaction, but the fact that Syria raised them indicated the regime's frustration and powerlessness in the severe crisis in which it was embroiled.[57]

In early May, 1967, another group of senior American officials came on a fact-finding mission to Israel and other states in the region. One of the leading personalities in the delegation was Roy Atherton, a top government official who had served in key posts connected to the Middle East and Israel. The delegation met with Foreign Ministry heads and senior IDF officers, who explained that despite the Syrians' saber-rattling it did not behave as though it was detached from reality, instead conducting a policy of brinksmanship. If tension began to soar, they would retreat and lower the flames a few degrees. They were continuously testing Israel's level of tolerance, cautiously and gradually, and assumed that sooner or later Israel would break under the heavy burden. The blow incurred by the Syrians on April 7 had not become a deterrent factor, and the Syrians resumed shooting at the Israelis who were farming the agricultural tracts the following day.[58]

Carried away by the victory euphoria and sense of unassailable superiority, the Israeli representatives proceeded to bluster defiantly. Even the Prime Minister, who generally muted his militant declarations, succumbed to the combative mood, announcing on May 11, 1967, that Israel would not hesitate employing its air power in response to Syrian aggression. The next day – the day that the Egyptian army began deploying in Sinai – the Israeli ambassador to the United States, Avraham Harman, reaffirmed Israel's resolve to act in the same format as April 7 if Syria persisted in its hostile conduct. Israel, he stressed, was gravely concerned over the terrorist activity being carried out from inside Syrian territory and Lebanon. The ambassador refused to reveal exactly how the Israeli government intended to respond, instead stressing that the regime in Damascus had to realize that it was not immune to a massive Israeli response, as its performance of April 7 had already proved. The Lebanese government would not enjoy neutral status, Harman cautioned, despite Israel's awareness that it had no interest in heating up the border.[59]

A State Department memo dated April 7 reported the air battle over the Golan Heights, noting that the aerial fight had begun after an hour-long exchange of fire along a wide swath of the Israeli–Syrian border. The memo also mentioned Israel's claim that there was nothing new in its activity in the demilitarized zones, and that it had previously cultivated the land there. Nevertheless, the Syrians had opened fire on the workmen. The memo went on to say that it accepted the validity of Israel's charges as opposed to Syria's. Both sides claimed victory.[60]

The memo's wording indicated the administration's indifference to the increasing border tension. In practical terms, the State Department's official announcement found it sufficient to express regret over the exchange of fire between Israel and Syria. According to another report from an administration official to Ambassador Harman, the former said that the president had reacted lightly to the air battle, adding that "Israel had [finally] taught them a lesson".[61]

A few days after the dogfight, the State Department began to come to life. Some circles in the administration feared that the increasing tension on the Israeli–Syrian border would imperil the stability of Jordan's Hashemite regime and the other Western interests in the region. Against this background, the State Department formulated a straightforward position on how to restore calm to the border. It released a memo stating that the administration accepted the UN position that Israel and Syria had to renew talks in the Israeli–Syrian Armistice Commission in order to reach a ceasefire. Until such an arrangement was found, Israel had to cease cultivating the lands under dispute.[62]

The American ambassador to Israel, Woolworth Barbour, exhibited a similar tendency to walk between the cracks on the issue of mounting border friction, speaking with great discretion and avoiding any expressions of anger or threats regarding Israel's military conduct. Just as we examined the administration's harsh condemnation of the Samu operation, we must also attempt to unravel the meaning behind Washington's silence over the deteriorating Israeli–Syrian relations.[63]

The ambassador was obliged to officially point out the administration's concern over the potential escalation of hostilities on the northern border and its consequences for the entire region. He asked that Israel halt its farming activity in the disputed areas, explaining that his request did not reflect an American stand on this specific issue nor was it by any means an expression of agreement with Syria's behavior. Washington simply wanted a cooling-off period along the border. The ambassador informed his listeners that Israel's supporters in the administration held a stronger position than that of the Arabists.[64]

In a talk with Moshe Bitan, a foreign ministry official, Barbour showed him a message that he received from the State Department instructing him to advise Israel to act with restraint and that the administration expected Israel not to take rush action. At this point the ambassador added his own astute interpretation of the message, placing emphasis upon the administration's hope that Israel would not act against Jordan and Lebanon.[65]

In other words, Washington was signaling to Israel that its official request for restraint and moderation was only obligatory lip service based on the United States' interest in maintaining an image of evenhandedness in the Arab–Israeli conflict. However, for all practical purposes, Israel could understand that the administration anticipated an Israeli strike against Syria, and would not obstruct Israel if it decided to embark on such an endeavor.[66]

From these reports, we may conclude with a significant degree of certainty that, during the months preceding the Six Day War, the Israeli military establishment assessed that the Johnson Administration, or at least key figures in it, would not oppose a military move against Syria even if they officially or publicly expressed reservations over it. This was, however, dependent on the strike being quick and crushing, an assessment that must have greatly influenced Israel's Syrian policy. Israel probably estimated that it had finally been given considerable latitude to carry out a military operation against the Syrians, and that the administration would neutralize Soviet intervention. This assessment was one of Israel's chief strategic assets in view of Jerusalem's swelling anxiety that Soviet involvement would countervail Israel's plans to scourge its northern foe.

The Policy of Escalation – A Missed Opportunity?

The escalation policy that Chief-of-Staff Rabin initiated and hoped to implement was designed to remove Syria from the cycle of hostilities against Israel. In our opinion, given the political-strategic circumstances of this period, the task was both justified and attainable. In the second half of the 1960s, Syria was the only state in the Middle East that still rejected the status quo created after the Sinai Campaign, and that wanted to forcibly turn back the clock. All of the other Arab countries – primarily Egypt and Jordan – were basically status-quo states. If they intended to change the current status in Israeli–Arab relations, they would not act forcefully, at least not in the foreseeable future. Israel, of course, had a supreme interest in safeguarding the status quo because of the strategic, security, political, and economic assets that it guaranteed.

Syria, on the other hand, was militarily weak. This was the main reason that it chose to fight Israel in a people's war, which it defined as the "weapon of the weak", and not in a full-scale con-frontation. Israel must have realized that a well-planned determined military assault on Syria would cause its swift demise. Simultaneously, Israel must have assumed that Egypt would stand out of the fray – militarily at least – if the offensive ended quickly and established solid facts on the ground. The available sources reveal that Washington and its allies in the Middle East – Jordan and Saudi Arabia, and of course Iran and Turkey – would have a hard time concealing their satisfaction over an Israeli initiative of this type against Syria.

However, the realization of a large-scale operation required a major strategic decision at the Eshkol-led political level. Our impression is that Rabin failed to convince the politicians of the wisdom and praxis of escalation, a policy that he hoped to implement together with his colleague David Elazar, CO Northern Command. Eshkol's wary and compromising nature must have inhibited him from making such an audacious and crucial decision. In addition, the Syrian regime's subdued reactions to the whipping it had recently suffered, especially the April 7 incident, may have led Eshkol towards the assumption that a full-scale military operation would be seen as an Israeli-initiated war that had nothing to do with self-defense. Thus, Eshkol must have feared that such a move would seriously stain Israel's good name as a peace-loving state that acted forcefully only when it came to the conclusion that all the paths to a political settlement had been blocked.[67]

In light of this situation, Rabin threatened to hand in his resignation if the political level refused to give the green light to the escalation policy and its final objective. In effect, this was what Moshe Dayan had done when he was Chief-of-Staff and felt that the Defense Minister, David Ben-Gurion, was dallying over approval of the continuation – let alone intensification – of the escalation policy that he, Dayan, had initiated. At the time, Dayan announced that under these circumstances he preferred to resign from his position. Rabin chose a different tack, instead opting to go "public" with his security doctrine. However, by doing so he made a serious tactical blunder. Eshkol was forced to distance himself from the idea of introducing regime change in Damascus via a military operation, and at the same time he also had to delegitimize the proposal by declaring it rash and illicit. The inevitable upshot was that Rabin proceeded with the escalation policy without the backing of the political level, without which the policy could not be implemented.[68]

In retrospect, we can only imagine what would have happened in the Middle East – especially in Israel – if the political level had taken heart and given the military apparatus the battle order to move against Syria. If the regime in Damascus had been "taken out", then a radical player "hell-bent" on destroying the status quo would have been removed from the region. Had this occurred, it is quite possible that the status quo would have led to circumstances more congenial for an Israeli–Egyptian dialogue toward a peace arrangement. Who knows? The pipedreams went up in smoke mainly because the Israeli leadership was unwilling to take responsibility for a far-reaching step, their indecisiveness creating a "vacuum" that compelled Egypt to act, as it understood its obligations. Military and political moves quickly catapulted the Middle East into the 1967 war that was followed by others which, all told, exacted a heavy price in human life and property.[69]

5

The Beginning of the Crisis – Perception of the Threat
Initial Stages

On April 11, 1967, Sidqi Mahmud, the Egyptian air force commander, arrived in Syria. The reason for the visit was the April 7 aerial clash in which six Syrian jet fighters were shot down. The Egyptians undoubtedly wanted to learn the details of the battle first hand and evaluate the Israeli air force's operational ability – perhaps with an eye to the approaching confrontation. Another issue discussed in the meeting was the quality of Syria's air defense system vis-à-vis the Israeli threat. Sidqi Suleiman, the Egyptian Prime Minister, came on the heels of the air force commander, landing in the Syrian capital on April 28.

This was the first visit by such a high-ranking Egyptian official since the dissolution of the UAR in 1961, therefore the visit may be viewed as a milestone in Egyptian–Syrian relations. Suleiman did not come to Damascus alone; accompanying him were Amin al-Hawadi, the minister of state, and Hasan Sabri al-Khouli, Nasser's personal envoy.[1]

One cannot overlook the possibility that these visits, and others (as well as diplomatic correspondence that had been, most probably, exchanged between the heads of both states), expressed a higher level of Egyptian–Syrian coordination in the pre-Six Day War period than what appeared on the surface. Indeed, reports from a senior official in the Jordanian government sent to the American administration shortly before the outbreak of the Six Day War revealed the closeness of Egyptian–Syrian coordination, especially at the military level. On May 21, 1967, for example, the Jordanian Chief-of-Staff, Ammar Khammash, informed the United States' ambassador to Jordan that Egypt had intentionally not summoned the joint Arab command because it wanted to maintain military coordination with Syria alone. King Hussein conveyed a similar report to the American ambassador.[2]

On May 15, 1967, Israel's Independence Day, an IDF parade was held in Jerusalem. The parade incurred scathing international criticism even though Israel had held similar parades in Jerusalem in the past. Eshkol's vacillation over the military event, combined with Ben-Gurion's heated criticism of Eshkol's lack of commitment to upgrade the status of Jerusalem as the capital city, seemed to have catapulted the question of Jerusalem's status to the forefront of the international agenda. Eshkol, as was his custom, attempted to walk between the cracks; he did not want to relinquish his image as a moderate and reasonable leader who would never engage his state in useless provocations against its rivals. On the other hand, he did not want to be portrayed as a weak and indecisive leader who could not defend the national interests of his state, foremost among them the status of Jerusalem.

Consequently Eshkol made a decision which would compromise these conflicting interests. He would hold the parade in Jerusalem on the condition that it was limited in size and with a minimum amount of weapons on display. This compromise, however, did not appear to satisfy the representatives of the Western powers. They opposed the very idea of a military parade being held in Jerusalem, and therefore informed Eshkol that they would not attend the review despite this compromise. The Israeli government was forced to express regret over their position. In a letter to Harold Wilson, the British Prime Minister, Eshkol communicated his disappointment at Britain's decision to condemn the parade despite its limited nature. Eshkol wrote that under these circumstances Israel should have staged a full-scale military parade.[3]

On May 14 and 15, 1967, Egyptian forces began to stream into Sinai. The move was carried out openly and was widely reported in the Egyptian media. Egyptian officials claimed that the troop concentrations were calculated to deter Israel from attacking Syria. Israel naturally interpreted the flagrancy of the Egyptian deployment as a provocation stemming from Egypt's vaunted sense of self-confidence. On May 15, 1967, the Israeli Chief-of-Staff, Yitzhak Rabin, sent a report to the commanding officer of Southern Command, Major General Yeshayahu Gavish. "We have reports," Rabin stressed, "that the Egyptian army is beginning to enter Sinai. I don't know exactly what this is all about but it's definitely more serious than anything we've experienced till now." Rabin proposed an immediate call-up of the reserves in order to deter the Egyptians from escalating the crisis. The Prime Minister, however, preferred to act with moderation and restraint at this stage, probably hoping that Nasser would be satisfied with his limited show of force and withdraw his troops back inside Egypt.[4]

Egypt did not, however, respond as Eshkol had hoped, instead choosing to enhance its militant moves. Parallel to the Egyptian military penetration into Sinai, their verbal provocations also grew more clamorous. Egypt accused Israel of planning an assault on Syria. The massive concentration of Egyptian troops in Sinai was intended to deter Israel from launching such an aggression. Egypt charged that if Israel were to carry out such an operation it would result in a head-on clash with Egypt. Also on that day, the Egyptian high command convened, headed by field marshal Abd al-Hakim Amer, first deputy to the Egyptian president and deputy commander of the armed forces. The high command decided to immediately dispatch the Chief-of-Staff, Gen. Mahmud Fawzi, to Syria.

That afternoon General Amer circulated a battle order describing the background to Egypt's moves. He placed special emphasis on the IDF troop concentrations on the Syrian front, which testified to the enemy's aggressive intentions, and on Egypt's obligation to deter Israel from an attack on an Arab country. Also on that day, a delegation of Egyptian parliament members headed by the chairman, Anwar al-Sadat, returned to Cairo after a lengthy visit to the Soviet Union. After the war, Nasser claimed that the delegation had returned with Soviet-obtained information on Israel's plans to attack Syria.[5]

On May 16, 1967, General Inder jit Rikhye, the commander of the UN forces in Sinai, was summoned to el-Arish and presented the Egyptian demand for the immediate evacuation of the UN Emergency Forces (UNEF) from Sinai that evening. The Egyptian Chief-of-Staff, General Fawzi, handed him a letter informing him of his order to the Egyptian army to prepare for immediate action against Israel if it attempts aggressive action against any Arab state. According to these orders, Fawzi stressed, the Egyptian army had entered Sinai. In order to guarantee the safety of UN forces deployed in strongholds along the border in Sinai, Fawzi urged Rikhye to instruct the United Nations' forces to withdraw from their positions immediately.[6]

Rikhye replied that he had to obtain instructions from U Thant, the UN secretary-general. The first assessment in UN circles was that the Egyptian demand did not mean a unilateral withdrawal of the UN troops from the entire peninsula but only from strategic points along the border. In order to clarify Egypt's intentions, the Under-Secretary-General of the UN, Ralph Bunche, invited the Egyptian ambassador to the UN, Mohammed Awed el Kony, for talks. Bunche apparently tried to limit the withdrawal of UN troops, a position rejected by the Secretary-General, who claimed that the UN forces were stationed in Sinai by Egyptian consent and that any demand for a change in their deployment would be regarded as a demand for a complete pullout.[7]

The UNEF had been stationed in Sinai as part of an arrangement that included the IDF's withdrawal from the peninsula after the Sinai Campaign. In early 1967 the UN force numbered 4300 soldiers from five countries: Sweden, Brazil, Canada, Yugoslavia, and India. Each country contributed one battalion, commanded by a staff with representatives from each of the countries. The overall commander was the Indian general, Rikhye, who was subordinate to the UN Secretary-General. The emergency force operated in two main sectors: the Gaza Strip and Sinai. The Swedish, Brazilian, and Indian battalions were stationed in Gaza and the Canadians and Yugoslavians in Sinai. Part of the Yugoslavian battalion was deployed in the Sharm el-Sheikh region to insure freedom of navigation through the Straits of Tiran.[8]

The Egyptians then tossed the ball into the Secretary-General's court. U Thant had to decide whether to accept the Egyptian demand and pull his forces out of Sinai, or enlist international support against such a move. On May 17, 1967, he met with the representatives of the countries whose forces were based in Sinai, making clear that Egypt was taking a highly irregular step and should have referred the matter directly to the Secretary-General, rather than General Rikhye. The general was unauthorized to approve of a partial withdrawal of troops and, according to U Thant, the Egyptian demand required a complete pullout. U Thant also informed them that the Yugoslavian units had already withdrawn from Sharm el-Sheikh, even before receiving UN instructions.[9]

On May 18, 1967, the Egyptian Foreign Minister, Mahmud Riad, sent a message to U Thant clarifying the Egyptian demand. Riad stressed that Egypt was determined to terminate the presence of the UNEF in Sinai and the Gaza Strip. Consequently it asked the UN to take the necessary steps to remove its forces from where they were stationed as early as possible. Egypt was well aware that its decision contradicted the "gentlemen's agreement" it had been party to since 1957, and that had been reached between the late Secretary-General, Dag Hammarskjöld, and President Nasser. This agreement stated that as a sovereign state Egypt had the undeniable right to demand the withdrawal of the UN forces, also including the understanding that Nasser would not make such a demand until the UN had determined that the force's mission was completed.[10]

After receiving Riad's letter, U Thant addressed the representatives of the countries whose soldiers comprised the UNEF, informing them that under the present circumstances nothing further could be done and that he had decided (as might be expected) to comply with the Egyptian demand and evacuate the UN troops from Sinai. In his report to the Security Council, the Secretary-General revealed that from the beginning of the crisis he had realized that the Egyptian demand left him no choice but to reply positively. Nevertheless, he stressed, he was taking this step with great sorrow.[11]

He later claimed that his decision had been based on both legal and practical considerations. In talks with Western officials, U Thant asserted that it was necessary to differentiate between the decision to evacuate the troops – a decision that was within his authority – and the decision to cancel the UNEF role in its entirety, which came under the jurisdiction of the General Assembly. The present case, he reasoned, had only been a matter of withdrawing the UN forces and not of eliminating their role, therefore his decision stood on a legal basis.[12]

The Secretary-General's decision was harshly denounced both in Israel and by the American administration. The main charge was that the UN chief had overstepped his legal mandate and proceeded unwisely in the political sphere. Legally he could have stated that the Egyptian demand would be discussed in the UN General Assembly because of the issue's momentous implications. By postponing implementation, he might have allowed the crisis to cool off, perhaps even freezing it for a long period. Israel claimed that such a *modus operandi* conformed to the understandings it had reached with Hammarskjöld after the Sinai Campaign. It also charged that the alacrity with which U Thant had agreed to

Egypt's demand to oust the UN left Egypt no choice but to pursue its escalatory measures – including closure of the Straits of Tiran – lest Egypt appear weak vis-à-vis Israel in the eyes of the world.

After the UN evacuation, Egyptian troops took control of the Sharm el-Sheikh region. Under these circumstances it was apparent that Egypt's announcement of the Straits' closure to Israeli shipping was only a matter of time. If Egypt would not undertake such a move now that the area was under its control, it would leave itself open to its enemies hounding recriminations that it conducts a cowardly foreign policy, exploiting the UN's presence in the region as a pretext to avoid taking stiff action against Israel. As expected, several days after the departure of the UN forces Egypt declared the Straits of Tiran closed to all ships flying the Israeli flag, and to all foreign vessels carrying strategic materials (weapons and fuel) bound for Israel. Israel termed Egypt's activity as a provocation and aggression, defining the closure of the Straits a *casus belli*. This was the setting for intensive political activity designed to temper the combustible atmosphere in the Mideast. When diplomacy failed, the Six Day War erupted on June 5, 1967.

The Egyptian Position

The Egyptian position during the crisis – in public announcements and diplomatic contacts – was characterized by a high degree of determination, galloping self-confidence, and brazenness on almost every issue. The Egyptians' braggadocio about the coming victory was highly publicized. The highest political level now expressed similar positions, and even bolder ones, both in limited forums and in talks with Western figures. For example, on May 16, 1967, in a meeting with the famed British General, Bernard Montgomery, the hero of the battle of Al-Alamein, Nasser pretended to ignore the crisis engulfing the Middle East by putting on a display of calmness and business as usual. He emphasized his desire to improve Egypt's relations with Britain, *inter alia*, by seeking a solution to the problem of Aden. Nasser's memory lapse was not accidental; in a conversation with the American envoy, Robert Anderson, a few days before the outbreak of war, he made a deliberate attempt to exude equanimity and self-confidence. He informed Anderson that he had knowledge (whose source is not clear) that Israel would launch the first strike. Nevertheless, he was certain that the outcome of the confrontation would be in Egypt's favor.[13]

Approximately two weeks before the war, CIA analysts studied Nasser's motives. They presented the president with a memo stating that over and above Nasser's fear of an Israeli operation against Syria, his decisions were based on the assumption that the Egyptian army was sufficiently prepared to absorb an Israeli first strike, though it might not be able to defeat Israel on the battlefield. The Johnson administration's heavy commitment to the Vietnam War, together with Egypt's plummeting economy and Nasser's belief in an American–Israeli plot against him, influenced his decision making. In addition, the memo noted that Nasser believed he had emerged from the first round of the crisis on top. Israel had been cornered into an agonizing dilemma in which each of the alternatives posed grave dangers. According to the memo, one possibility for Israel to get out of this complication might be to attack Syria, forcing Egypt to face a debilitating dilemma itself: either avoid responding and forfeit its prestige and credibility, or make a move under circumstances lacking the element of surprise.[14]

The Egyptians insisted that Israel and the United States were to blame for the crisis. Egyptian spokesmen charged that the crisis had erupted because the Eshkol government intended to topple the Damascus regime by launching a major military operation against Syria. The Egyptians alleged that this action had been coordinated with, and backed by, the White House. Egypt, they stressed to their Western listeners, had learned of Israel's intentions from independent sources, not Soviet ones as Israeli and American representatives claimed. Thus, we may assume that Egypt did not wish to completely refute the claims that it had received information of Israel's aggressive plans from Soviet sources, instead wanting to make clear that its knowledge had been obtained from its own sources as well.[15]

The Egyptians considered the United States just as culpable as Israel was in the breakout of the crisis. The US was accused on two counts: first, Washington's overall responsibility for the establishment of the State of Israel and the generous assistance it extended to it. This aid had supposedly encouraged Israel to develop an aggressive policy toward the Arab world over the years. The second charge was related to the administration's responsibility for the outbreak of the present crisis. The Egyptians claimed that even before the crisis the United States had promised Israel that the sixth fleet – cruising in the Mediterranean – would come to its defense if necessary. As a result, the Egyptian spokesmen emphasized that Israel's self-confidence had increased, and that it had begun plotting against its neighbors, Syria in particular. Once the crisis developed Washington displayed nearly total support for Israel, putting itself on a collision course with Egypt and the entire Arab world. Similar charges were also raised by Syrian officials to Western representatives.[16]

Not only was the United States guilty of abetting Israel's instigative policy toward the Arabs, it was also accused by high-ranking Egyptian officials of attempting to replace the current regime in Egypt, including President Nasser. A few months before the war, the American ambassador to Egypt had reported that almost all of the senior officials in Egypt believed the rumors that the CIA was planning to cripple the Egyptian regime. Some Egyptians, the ambassador noted, felt that the CIA was carrying out an independent policy of which other figures in the administration were unaware. Mahmud Riad, the Egyptian Foreign Minister, made a similar charge to the American ambassador. Nasser, too, raised this issue in a supposedly off-handed fashion with Secretary-General U Thant, telling him that he regretted being unable to attend the conference of the heads of African states that would be held in Kinshasa in August 1967. The reason was his fear that the CIA would try to assassinate him there.[17]

Referring to Egypt's decision to block the Straits of Tiran, the Egyptian representatives reaffirmed both publicly and privately that this was a decision taken by an independent state, concerning an area under its full sovereignty. The Egyptian leaders stressed that no country – not even the United States – would dictate to Egypt how to conduct its affairs in its sovereign territory. Egypt announced that it would halt Israeli vessels and impound strategic cargoes, especially oil, that was destined for Israel. Egyptian spokesmen warned that if American warships tried to pass through the Straits and break the embargo forcefully, Egypt would not hesitate to open fire.[18]

Egypt claimed, *inter alia*, that since it was in a state of war with Israel it had the legal right to block the Straits. It also asserted that Israel had taken control of the port of Eilat *after* the Armistice Agreement with Egypt had been signed on February 24, 1949, which was in flagrant violation of the agreement. Therefore, Israel's control of the port was illegal. Finally, Egypt attempted to use the precedent of the United States maritime embargo on Cuba during the October 1962 missile crisis to prove its legitimacy. Egypt's message was loud and clear; what the US had done when it was not in a state of war, Egypt could certainly do, because in its eyes it was in a state of war.[19]

At the same time as Egypt expressed unwavering determination on preventing Israeli navigation through the Straits, its representatives tried to scatter a smoke screen and give the impression that Israel, not Egypt, was the party that had toppled the deck and disturbed the status quo. According to Nasser's spokesmen, Egypt's only goal was to return the situation to its state prior the 1956 Sinai Campaign. This formula, as mentioned, was intended to grant the Egyptian move a veneer of legitimacy. It implied that responsibility for the change in the status quo lay with Israel because of its martial activity, the Sinai Campaign, which had granted her free navigation through the Straits of Tiran. Egypt only wanted to restore the region to its previous state by annulling the consequences of Israel's warlike conduct.[20]

The repeated use of this formula may also have meant to imply a rather practical, moderate Egyptian position. Although Egypt declared an embargo it did not really intend to implement it for any length of time. It would therefore demonstrate its irrefutable sovereignty over the Straits and its readiness to confront both Israel and the United States. Also, by such a step Egypt could avoid any confrontation with Israel. This assessment is supported by statements from a senior Soviet official to American diplomats: "It's true that Nasser declared the Straits closed, but in practice he didn't close them." For this reason, the Soviet official asked the Americans not to demand Nasser to officially announce that he would avoid blocking the Straits, since such a move would badly mar his prestige and status. The Soviets hoped that Washington would take steps to help Nasser refrain from putting his threat to the test.[21]

As part of Egypt's effort to evince moderation and willingness to comply with the many countries asking it to do everything possible to avert a confrontation in the region, the Egyptian spokesmen gave a non-committal – but not entirely negative – response to the proposal to refer the question of Israeli navigation in the Straits of Tiran to a neutral third party. Nasser expressed his reservations, though not necessarily opposition, to the idea of referring the matter to the UN, claiming that it mattered little since Israel attached negligible importance to UN decisions and refused to implement them. It was doubtful, therefore, that Israel would agree to a decision that would work in Egypt's favor. On the other hand, the Egyptian ambassador to the United States, Mustafa Kemal, gave guarded support to the idea.[22]

Nasser displayed a more positive attitude to the proposal to hand the matter to the International Court of Justice in The Hague, a proposal that was Johnson's initiative. The president asked the envoy Robert Anderson to convey the proposal to Nasser and tell him that if he agreed to transfer the issue of maritime freedom to the international court, he would create an atmosphere that would enable the United States to help him on other matters. Nasser informed Anderson that he was prepared to seriously consider the proposal.[23]

The Egyptians did not completely reject a number of other proposals, including its willingness to implement the embargo with a flexible interpretation of the term "strategic materials" destined for Israel. Egyptian officials indicated a possibility on Egypt's part to adopt the list of "strategic goods" accepted by the United States in the *United States Act of Battle – list of strategic materials*. Oil did not appear on the list as "strategic material". The Egyptian representatives also expressed an openness to examine the possibility of Egypt's consent to the passage of oil to Israel on vessels carrying foreign flags – if the oil was limited to civilian needs, and not one drop more.[24]

Another Egyptian position that was formulated at the highest level of state and presented as an expression of Egypt's moderation and interest in finding a political solution to the crisis was the Egyptian commitment not to be the side to fire the first shot in the war. President Nasser and Foreign Minister Riad dwelled on this position and made it clear that Egypt was prepared to absorb the first strike if an Israeli attack appeared imminent. It is important to recall that up until the outbreak of the war, American strategic analysts assumed that Egypt's military deployment in Sinai was defensive in nature.[25]

In retrospect, and in light of the devastation to the Egyptian army in Israel's preemptive strike, Egypt's position brings to mind a sense of self-sacrifice. By promising to forego the first strike, Egypt apparently hoped to deny Israel's use of it. Certainly,

Egypt's interests were being served the longer the Straits remained closed and the more deeply Egyptian forces were entrenched in Sinai, a situation that squeezed Israel into an impossible situation. Egypt's guarantee not to launch a pre-emptive strike made it difficult for Israel to take such a step. In the absence of such a move Israel would soon find itself facing a new status quo, while its ability to introduce changes was increasingly diminished. Such a scenario portended an ignominious setback without Egypt having fired a single shot.[26]

Aharon Yariv, the Israeli chief of intelligence, gave a lecture in which he quoted from his Egyptian counterpart during the war, Selah a-din al-Heidi. From his statement one may conclude that Egypt's commitments not to launch the first strike were based on the view that Egypt could absorb an Israeli preemptive strike. On May 25/26, 1967, Hadidi said: "We were called to a general staff meeting attended by the president of the state [Nasser]." A debate ensued between the president and the air force commander. Nasser said: "It's done; we've made the decision not to launch the first strike", to which the air commander replied that if the "Jews" attacked first, Egypt's situation would be completely changed. Nasser's response was that "this is a political decision, and the military is supposed to carry it out". The same argument was repeated on May 26, 1967, and June 2, 1967. The Egyptian air force was ordered not to launch the first strike.[27]

Whatever the Egyptian motives may have been, one thing is certain: Egypt's position reflects the enormous self-confidence felt by the leadership on the outcome of a clash with Israel. Nasser gave conspicuous expression to this inner strength in a speech on May 26, 1967, where he highlighted the revolutionary change in Egypt's position on a military confrontation with Israel and its ultimate objective: "We've been waiting for the day when we are ready for battle," he thrilled his listeners. He continued, "recently we have felt that our strength is sufficient, and that if we engage in combat, then, with the help of god, we will emerge victorious. The seizure of Sharm el-Sheikh means war with Israel, and we are prepared to enter an all-out battle . . . The struggle with Israel will be total; its basic goal will be the destruction of Israel. I would not say this five or even three years ago. Today I say it because I'm certain of it."[28]

Another probable explanation for Egypt's position is that it relied too heavily on American assessments, according to which

Israel would not dare open hostilities without Washington's backing. The White House had made it clear to Egypt that not only had it not given Israel the green light for a military operation, but that it had made every effort to deter it from such a move. It should be noted that an Egyptian foreign ministry memo assessed that Israel would not embark upon war against Egypt in the absence of American backing, and that "all signs indicate that Israel is at present unprepared to initiate a campaign single-handedly against Egypt". The likelihood of Israeli military involvement, Egyptian officials reported, depended primarily on the support of superpowers outside the region. [29]

At this stage it was doubtful whether Israel would receive the backing it needed, as a basic disagreement existed among the Western superpowers concerning how to deal with the crisis. France wanted to remove itself as far as possible from military involvement in the conflict. When the United States weighed the possibility of intervention on Israel's behalf, it had to acknowledge the Soviet Union's bitter condemnation, the closure of the Suez Canal and its ramifications for the West, an Egyptian military response against American targets, damage to Western oil sources, and a vast uprising in the Arab world against the US.[30]

The Egyptians may have presumed that even if Israel initiated an attack, it would be a limited action that Egypt could easily absorb and afterwards, from a superior position, engage in negotiations for some kind of an arrangement. Although there is no conclusive evidence, it is reasonable to assume that the Egyptians may have believed that after the limited Israeli attack, Egypt would enter negotiations during which it could propose the reopening of the Straits of Tiran in exchange for close international monitoring of Israel's nuclear activity. Another possibility that should not be dismissed is that Egyptian willingness to consider various proposals was merely a deception to lull Israel into lowering its guard, and that Egypt really intended to launch a surprise attack as it rapidly converted from a defensive layout to war deployment.

Is Egypt Heading for a War?

The military–political crisis that erupted just prior to the Six Day War came as a complete surprise to Israel. In the prewar period, official assessment analysts in Israel held that Egypt had been aware of its military inferiority vis-à-vis Israel since the Sinai Campaign, and was therefore avoiding taking steps that might lead to a confrontation in the foreseeable future. Egypt would continue in this direction even if it meant reneging on its commitment to the pan-Arab cause and its Syrian ally.[31]

The Israeli situation assessment was heavily based upon the fact that the highest levels of Egyptian leadership, including Nasser, had repeatedly stated both publicly and discreetly that Egypt wished to avoid a military conflict with Israel, and would not allow militant elements in the Arab world to drag it into war. These statements could only be interpreted as an admission of Egypt's political and military weakness vis-à-vis Israel. In May 1967, no new circumstances had developed that required altering this assessment.[32]

As stated, in mid-1967 Israel saw no reason to change its situation estimate regarding the likelihood of war breaking out in the region. There were no signs that Egypt had revised its assessment – which it adopted after the Sinai Campaign – of the balance of forces between Israel and the Arab states. Egypt still believed that it was strategically inferior to Israel. Much of the Egyptian army was still in Yemen; border incidents with Syria had become routine and did not seem to call for a change in the customary Egyptian response: condemning Israel, while shunning steps that might lead to a military clash. In sum, all signs indicated that this situation would continue for many years to come.

The concentration of Egyptian forces in Sinai, the ousting of the UN forces from Sinai, and above all, the closure of the Straits of Tiran to Israeli vessels and foreign ships carrying "strategic material" to Israel symbolized an unexpected and perilous turning point in Egypt's position. The head of Israeli intelligence, Aharon Yariv, estimated shortly before the outbreak of the war that the Egyptian move was planned to create a new territorial reality in the Middle East, a reality totally unlike that which had existed after the 1948 war and the signing of the Armistice Agreements. "Nasser," he stated (and it is difficult to know on what evidence) apparently intended to return Israel to what many had termed "its natural proportions," that is, the 1947 partition borders as determined by the UN partition plan. This would be achieved by political moves alongside military and paramilitary ones.[33]

All of these developments underscored the intelligence failure that characterized the waiting period. When the newly appointed

Defense Minister, Moshe Dayan, showed up at the Knesset's Foreign Affairs & Defense Committee shortly after the war, he enumerated five situation estimates that had dominated the prewar period and had been proven wrong during the crisis. In the heat of the euphoria that pervaded the entire country in the wake of the dazzling victory, no one thought of demanding an investigation into the reasons for the intelligence establishment's shortcomings. These are just several examples of Israeli intelligence deficiencies: (a) Egypt did not feel that its commitment to respond to IDF actions against Syria and Fatah terrorists in Jordan warranted Egyptian military operations against Israel; (b) Since Egypt was deeply involved in a civil war in Yemen, it would be incapable of opening a second front against Israel; and (c) Cairo did not take Jordan's criticism of its restriction of Israeli freedom through the Straits of Tiran seriously. Israeli intelligence believed as late as the third week in May that the entry of the Egyptian army into Sinai was only saber-rattling, and that Nasser did not really intend to initiate a war against Israel. Egypt would have trouble removing the UNEF, especially from Sharm el-Sheikh.[34]

Given the accepted intelligence estimate stating that Egypt had no plans to engage in a military confrontation, the Israeli leadership suddenly faced surprising developments with Egypt's provocative steps. Egypt must have been aware of their grave implications and accepted the likelihood of a massive Israeli military response. Against this background, Israeli assessment analysts and the national leadership found it difficult to devise concrete answers to the new reality. In the absence of conclusive answers, Israel's leaders struggled to plot out a clear-cut resolute policy. To make this possible, the following questions had to be immediately addressed:

- Was Egypt's retraction of its policy to keep the conflict in cold storage – that had been in effect since the Sinai Campaign – final and irreversible?
- What caused this volte-face? Did Egypt really believe Israel intended to attack Syria, or was this allegation designed to justify a warlike move whose goals went beyond the defense of Syria?
- Had Egypt succeeded in secretly developing or acquiring advanced weapons systems that gave it a sense of superiority in the balance of forces?

- Had the Soviet Union promised Egypt political-military support in the event of a regional flare-up?
- Was there a strong likelihood that Egypt would initiate a military strike against Israel that included a massive attack against strategic targets and population centers?
- What was Washington's position on the crisis? Would it stand behind the guarantees it had given Israel publicly and secretly? Would the United States go along with an Israeli-initiated military operation?

As stated, Israel was struggling to come up with clear-cut answers to these and other questions. In the initial stages of the crisis it was obvious that Israel did not take the Egyptian moves in Sinai too seriously; certainly not as an immediate existential danger. In our opinion, among other things that contributed to this perspective was the fact that the concentration of Egyptian forces in Sinai had been carried out openly and arrogantly. It was assumed that if a state was planning a military operation against its neighbor it would do so with subterfuge. Israeli analysts probably estimated that Egypt would be satisfied with flexing its muscles to improve its status in the Arab world, but would not go any further. The fact that the Soviet Union exhibited restraint and moderation in its initial responses, and in its official contacts with Israel had tried to present a sense of business as usual, must have contributed to Israel's relatively sanguine estimate at this point.

At a meeting in the Chief-of-Staff's office on the morning of May 16, 1967, Yitzhak Rabin stated that the Egyptians had entered Sinai in order to obstruct the IDF's freedom of movement in the north, thereby deterring Israel from attacking Syria. Rabin declared that due to this development the IDF would now have to deploy on the southern border in order to retain its freedom of action in the north. Despite this, he still doubted that Egypt's military movements posed a real threat to Israel. At the end of the discussion, it was decided to beef up the IDF in the south, putting the troops on alert for additional reinforcing. The commanding officer of the southern command, Yeshayahu Gavish, felt that the number of forces under his command was insufficient. Therefore, he demanded more troops and the permission to advance them to the border, rather than leaving them on stand-by in their home bases.[35]

At a GHQ meeting on May 17, 1967, the chief of intelligence

gave his assessment of the Egyptian moves. His main points were that at present the Syrians considered an Israeli attack imminent and had conveyed this estimate to the Egyptians. Under these circumstances, the two Arab states had reached the conclusion that Israel was planning a large-scale ground assault against Syria. Egypt calculated that its military activity in Sinai would force the superpowers to pressure Israel to call off its aggressive plans against Syria. Simultaneously, Egypt also believed its diplomatic and military maneuvering would elevate its status in the Arab world. On the basis of this appraisal, and despite Israeli intelligence's estimate that Egypt wanted to avoid a military clash, the Chief-of-Staff announced that the IDF would be taking precautionary steps for any unexpected developments. The Egyptian moves had created a new situation, regardless of their original intention.[36]

On May 18, 1967, in a talk between the United States' ambassador to Israel and the head of Israeli intelligence's research division, Shlomo Gazit, the latter presented a relatively confident estimate of the Egyptian moves. What Egypt wants, Gazit said to the ambassador, "is not a real factor for Israel". Israel's primary concern was the terrorist activity on the Syrian border. According to Gazit, Israeli intelligence estimated that Egypt still preferred to avoid a military confrontation with Israel. Nasser was and remained a consummate realist in everything connected to his relations with Israel. Gazit pointed out that Egypt had been compelled to take these steps in order to demonstrate its willingness to defend a fellow Arab state. The Israeli intelligence expert did not believe that this would lead to a belligerent showdown. Although the evacuation of the UN forces from Sinai had complicated the situation, everything still remained part of an elaborate Egyptian charade. A similar estimate was conveyed to the British ambassador to Israel.[37]

Would the US Stand by its Commitments to Israel?

Available documents reveal that the Johnson administration – much like Israel – lacked a comprehensive picture of Nasser's intentions and was unsure whether Egypt's moves were "serious" and part of a larger plan, or designed solely for show. At any rate, Washington was certain that Nasser's allegations regarding IDF troop concentrations in the north were unsubstantiated. However, there were differing opinions in the Johnson Administration concerning whether Nasser should be informed that his conviction of an impending Israeli assault on Syria was without basis. In the end, the decision was made not to inform him. The main reason for this was the fear that Israel would attack Syria; if that happened the Arab world would be furious with the United States and accuse it of military collusion with Israel. President Johnson considered sending vice-president Hubert Humphrey to the Middle East in a last ditch effort to halt the descent to war and the erosion of America's status in the Arab world.[38]

In the first stages of the crisis, Israel set in motion an intense diplomatic campaign to convince the UN apparatus of the fallacy in the claims that IDF troops had been concentrated on the Syrian border. On May 15, 1967, Foreign Minister Abba Eban instructed the Israeli ambassador to the UN, Gideon Raphael, to inform UN Under-Secretary-General Ralph Bunche that the IDF was not amassed along the Syrian border, and that as long as quiet was maintained on the Israeli side it would rein on the Syrian side as well. Raphael reported to Eban that Bunche had told him that the UN forces had corroborated the Israeli version. According to Bunche, U Thant conveyed this information to Egypt's representative in the UN. In addition, Bunche himself had spoken with the Egyptian delegate on this matter. And finally, United States intelligence services confirmed that the charge that Israel had concentrated its forces on the northern border was false.[39]

Israel sought another course in dealing with the UN machinery, attempting to convince the UN to adopt a "foot-dragging" tactic in the evacuation of its forces. Israel suggested that U Thant would try to buy time by claiming that the removal of UN troops from Sinai entailed logistical and legal details that required time to work out. Israel's leaders hoped that the crisis would cool off as time passed. Consequently, Egypt would pull its forces out of Sinai, and the UN troops would remain in their positions. At the same time, Egypt might chalk up prestige points as the party that assisted an Arab state threatened by Israel, and that succeeded in preventing the enemy from realizing its aggressive plans.[40]

Israel made various claims to convince as many states as possible, as well as the UN Secretary-General himself, that the evacuation of the UN forces would upset regional stability. The Secretary-General did not possess the legal authority to make this decision alone. In a letter to U Thant, Eban reminded him that for eleven years UN forces have been a balancing force in the Middle East. He also stressed that his predecessor, Dag Hammarskjöld, made it clear that if a demand were made to withdraw the UN forces, he would bring the matter to a discussion in broad international forums while examining the implications of such a step. Israel, Eban stated, was deeply concerned over the grave consequences of an impulsive UN pullout from Sinai.[41]

Following this, the Israeli ambassador to the UN, Gideon Raphael, received instructions to inform Ralph Bunche that the UNEF had been stationed in Sinai as a buffer to prevent hostilities from erupting between Israel and Egypt. Now, when Egypt was pouring its forces into the peninsula and the danger of a full-scale confrontation appeared imminent, the UN was facing the test of a highly dangerous reality. Bunche replied that the Secretary-General had instructed the commander of the UN forces in Sinai, General Rhikye, to inform the Egyptians that he receives orders only from the Secretary-General and not from any Egyptian element. U Thant also stated that any violation of the UN forces' freedom of action was an expression of Egypt's non-compliance with the continuation of the force's activity in general, and could result in the complete removal of the force from Sinai. Bunche explained that the Secretary-General was aware that the evacuation might lead to a military confrontation. Nevertheless, he had obtained a legal ruling stating that the continued presence of the UNEF in Sinai depended on the host state, Egypt.[42]

Parallel to this, Israel's attitude toward the continued presence of the UN troops was intended to avoid creating the impression that Israel was frightened and pleading for its life. Israel wanted to demonstrate its interest in seeing the UN remain in Sinai, however at the same time it did not want to appear dependent on the UN forces to protect it from Egyptian aggression. Israel had the power to face any Egyptian challenge and defeat any state in the region that sought to destroy it. Israel was not interested in flaunting its power, but in preserving stability. An armed clash would serve neither side's interests – even if Israel was certain of victory.

An outstanding expression of this trend appeared in a confidential message that Eshkol sent to Ambassador Raphael, instructing him to propose to the Secretary-General that he visit Israel and Egypt. The proposal must have been intended to gain time, in the hope that passions would abate and a quiet political solution to the crisis worked out. Nevertheless, Eshkol admonished the ambassador that under no circumstances should it be found out that Israel had initiated the visit. Eshkol was worried that the initiative might be interpreted as an expression of cowardice and the wish to eschew a military showdown at all costs.[43]

Already in the early stages of the crisis Israel sent the American administration clarifications and assessments on the background of the ordeal and Israel's position. The following points were emphasized: (a) Israel had not concentrated its forces on the Syrian border; (b) as long as no shooting incidents broke out, there was absolutely no cause for alarm over an Israeli attack on Syria; (c) Israel believes that Syria wants to entangle Egypt in a war with Israel; (d) Egyptian military activity, especially the concentration of Egyptian forces in Sinai, encourages Syria to continue violent activity against Israel; (e) Israel let Washington know that it was not averse to having this information passed on to the Egyptians.[44]

Indeed, the administration quickly transmitted the Israeli views to senior figures in the Egyptian regime, also making clear to Egypt that United States intelligence agencies had no evidence of any special change in IDF troop deployment on the northern border. The American officials stressed that they were in contact with Israel at the highest level (President Johnson's message to Prime Minister Eshkol on May 17, 1967), and had demanded that both Israel and Egypt exhibit restraint. In addition, Egypt was asked to exert its influence on Damascus so that Syria would proceed with prudence, but it appears that these exhortations fell short of the mark.[45]

The entry of Egyptian forces into Sinai, especially their takeover of the Sharm el-Sheikh region, awakened the Americans to the realization that Israel would probably attack the Egyptian army. Consequently, Johnson sent an urgent message to Eshkol on May 17, 1967, expressing the United States' understanding of the difficult situation of having neighboring states that are constantly testing the patience of Israel. Despite this, Johnson's sympathy for Israel's plight did not translate into practical support; instead he was keenly interested in limiting Israel's moves and preventing Israel from realizing its natural right to self-defense. Johnson stressed "in the strongest terms" that Israel had to avoid actions that would aggravate the tension in the region.[46]

The message also demanded that Israel keep in close consultation with its main friends, primarily the United States. In other words, the president was ordering Israel to avoid taking steps without prior agreement from the US. Finally, so as to leave no room for doubt about the administration's seriousness, Johnson concluded his letter with an outright warning to Israel (that Rusk had recommended) not to take any unilateral military steps; otherwise it would risk losing America's commitment of protection. "I am certain," he wrote to Eshkol, "that you will understand that I cannot accept any responsibility on behalf of the United States which arises as the result of actions that we have not been consulted on."[47]

The president's message must have been very disconcerting for Israel. It completely ignored the assurance of maritime freedom in the Straits of Tiran that the US had given Israel following the Sinai Campaign. The message also failed to mention that over the years former presidents had promised Israeli governments a series of guarantees for its sovereignty and territorial integrity, in case of a threat to its existence and to its freedom of navigation in the Straits of Tiran.[48]

Considering Israel's deep interest in American security guarantees, it is hardly surprising that Israel was very disappointed with the president's message. Since assuming office following Kennedy's assassination, Johnson had made every effort to demonstrate friendship to Israel – both verbally and practically. He approved the sale of tanks and Skyhawk fighters, and was the first president to invite an Israeli Prime Minister on an official visit to the United States (June 1964). Thus, many people in Israel expected Johnson to sustain the spirit of this friendship by extending support to Israel in the face of Egypt's military provocations.

Johnson, however, chose a path designed to forestall an Arab–Israeli confrontation at all costs. He was correct in his assumption that the US was capable of exerting very little pressure on Egypt because of Cairo's close ties with the Soviet Union. For this reason he channeled the brunt of American pressure on Israel and, in straightforward terms, demanded that it refrain from a military response at this point.[49]

The president's message expressed a serious downturn in the administration's attitude toward Israel at this strenuous hour. Not only had the president backtracked on his country's commitments regarding Israel's territorial integrity and maritime freedom in the Straits, he also denied it the right to respond to the immediate threats to its existence. Eban correctly defined these positions as reflecting the president's "new policy". In a conversation with

Ambassador Barbour a day after the message had arrived, Eban stressed that the United States' request that Israel consult with it before responding to Egyptian provocation was, in effect, an American dictate.[50]

So as to reemphasize the seriousness of the United States' demand, Under-Secretary of State Eugene Rostow added oral clarifications to the president's message. Speaking with the Israeli ambassador to the United States, Avraham Harman, the American under-secretary asked him to convey a point-blank warning to his government – not to attack the Egyptians stationed in Sharm el-Sheikh.[51]

A memo written after the war surveyed US positions vis-à-vis the crisis during this period of time, stating that the administration's first major decision in the crisis had been to deter Israel from seeking a military solution. The memo included an interesting sideline: certain circles in the administration thought that Israel should be allowed to act as it saw fit, but this opinion had been almost totally rebuffed for the following reasons:

1. First, the administration estimated that the US had a genuine interest in averting a major war in the Middle East.
2. Second, certain circles within the administration feared that Israel might suffer disastrously, causing the United States to feel obligated to come to its assistance. Such a move would seriously compromise America's relations with the Arab world.
3. Furthermore, the US was currently heavily committed to the war in Vietnam and was therefore highly opposed to the possibility of being engaged in another military confrontation.
4. Lastly, a military confrontation would probably offset the chances of an Arab–Israeli political arrangement in the future.[52]

The memo stressed that there were other views within the administration regarding the positions the United States should adopt in the crisis. One view was that Israel should be allowed to exert its military power because its survival was at stake. The supporters of this view stressed that any government that found itself in such a situation – including the United States – would consider acting with force in order to guarantee its basic interests. With an astonishing degree of candor (rare in official American correspondence), the memo stated that the US criticized Israel's retaliation policy but at no point proposed a better one. The memo mentioned Israel's doubt as to whether the Johnson Administration was capable of resolving the crisis in a peaceable manner, and it seems that the president himself had some doubts too.[53]

In any case, Eshkol fully understood the message's bottom line, answering Johnson in a long detailed letter that reflected the Prime Minister's customary style of cautious maneuvering. On the one hand, he wanted to inform Johnson of Israel's dismay that the message had ignored the United States' commitments to Israel, trying to limit Israel's freedom of action at this anxiety-ridden hour. On the other hand, Eshkol could not overlook the fact that the message had been sent from the highest level of government – from the president himself – and the prestige of that position. Eshkol's reply was therefore intended to show respect for the president's office and to avoid provoking him, as this would put Israel in an unfavorable position.[54]

Eshkol implied that Syria and its policy remained the focus of Israel's concern at this stage. Eshkol began his message by stating that the main factor in the crisis was Syria's terroristic policy. The Israeli government had displayed notable self-control in recent weeks in the face of Syrian provocations. Eshkol also referred indirectly, but critically, to the president's demand that Israel continue to keep showing restraint, by pointing out that the crisis would not be solved by Israel's indefinite postponement of a military response.[55]

Eshkol further stressed that Israel had information that many of the terrorist acts emanating from Jordan and Lebanon had been prompted by Syria. Their aim had been to push these countries onto a collision course with Israel, who refused to play by Syria's rules. Eshkol probably hoped to make the president realize that Israel would not repeat the mistake of late 1966, when it carried out a heavy-handed military retaliation (the Samu Operation) against Jordan, a prominent pro-Western state, thereby infuriating Washington. Eshkol must have calculated that by focusing Israel's reaction on a pro-Soviet regime like the one in Damascus he would increase American support of Israel and its military plans.[56]

Eshkol devoted the second part of his message to the threat created by the entry of Egyptian forces into Sinai (which now included four divisions and six hundred tanks). This deployment,

Eshkol stressed, was totally unwarranted. Egypt was undoubtedly aware that Israel had not amassed its troops on the Syrian border, as it had received verifications of this from the UN and other American sources. Nevertheless, Egypt continued to build up its layout in Sinai, a development that naturally forced Israel to take precautionary steps and reinforce its troops in the south. Again, Eshkol was rolling the ball into Syria's court. The entrance of the Egyptian army into Sinai, he admonished, was liable to encourage Syria to persist in its policy of terrorism, since Egypt's backing could be interpreted as pan-Arab support of Syria's aggressive conduct. The only way to stave off escalation was to restore the situation to its previous state.[57]

The Israeli message also reaffirmed that it would be most unfortunate if the UN demonstrated irresolution regarding its deployment of forces in Sinai. The UN's mission, the message stressed, was not to evacuate the peninsula so that one side could act aggressively toward the other. Israel hoped that the Secretary-General would refuse to comply with a change in the status quo until he received a mandate for this from the General Assembly. Referring to the way the US responded to the aggressive Egyptian moves, Eshkol chose to cautiously criticize the Johnson administration and its intent to shun the commitments the United States had made towards Israel after the Sinai Campaign.[58]

At this time, Eshkol recalled that Israel had agreed to take enormous long-range risks, based on the American initiative that had led to the withdrawal of Israeli forces from Sinai and the Gaza Strip. Israel had submitted to the American demand, *inter alia*, because of the guarantee that UN forces would be stationed in Sinai as a buffer between Israel and Egypt. Basically, Eshkol's message said that it was unthinkable that in the present crisis the administration would renege on the arrangement it had initiated a decade ago. On the agenda was not just the UN's handling of the situation (Israel never had high expectations from that international body), but most importantly the credibility of American commitments. If the US would not remain firm regarding its guarantees to Israel, then who would believe that it would stand by its assurances in other cases.[59]

Referring to Israel's expectations of the American administration, Eshkol subtly urged the White House to reevaluate the wisdom of its present policies in the crisis. He implied that the administration should not delude itself into thinking that by embarking on an unbalanced policy in the crisis and exerting unconscionable pressure on Israel to abstain from exercising its natural right to self-defense, it would enhance the chances of a peaceful settlement of the crisis. This policy, he stressed, would only work to the detriment of both parties, encouraging President Nasser to undertake a much more militant policy in the crisis, which would inevitably result in a large-scale military clash.[60]

Since Egypt and Syria believed that Russian support was guaranteed, Eshkol emphasized that they felt no need to act with restraint. Here again, Eshkol implied that if the United States thought that its adoption of a neutral position in the crisis would advance a peaceful settlement, it was badly mistaken. It would only encourage the radical Arab regimes to escalate the crisis. Eshkol proposed that Washington clearly inform the Soviet leaders in the clearest of terms that the US was unconditionally obligated to protect Israel's security. Eshkol's message suggested that if the Soviet Union realized that the United States was backing Israel then there was a chance that the Soviet Union would use its influence to curb Egypt and Syria, prohibiting them from escalating the situation. Eshkol highlighted that this step was of momentous significance, and a basic formula for resolving the crisis.[61]

Eshkol concluded his message with a reminder to the president that in addition to the Eisenhower administration's commitment to Israel after the Sinai Campaign, all the American administrations since then – including Johnson's – had promised to protect Israel's sovereignty and territorial integrity. These guarantees were given at the highest level of office, that is, at the presidential level. Eshkol also recalled Johnson's statements in talks between the two leaders in June 1964, when the president had praised Israel and explicitly promised to stand by its side in case of a serious threat. As a close ally, Eshkol pointed out that Israel sympathized with the complexities of the United States' position at this time and its discomfort at being bound to measures that Israel might take without prior consultation. However, in light of the Egyptian troop concentrations and the ongoing terrorist activity on the northern border, America was first of all obligated to reaffirm its commitments to Israel.[62]

The Prime Minister's message to Johnson shows that as late as May 17–18, 1967, the Israelis did not consider the entry of Egyptian forces a major threat. Rather, it was seen as a demonstration of power designed to illustrate Egypt's preeminent position in the Arab world, and its ability to deter Israel from a military operation against a fellow Arab state. Israel probably hoped that its avoidance of highlighting Egypt's provocative steps would enable the Egyptians to return the situation to its previous state without detracting from their prestige. Eshkol purposely referred to Syria's terror policy in the beginning of his letter, only later mentioning the problem of Egyptian troops in Sinai. This attempt to downplay the situation was also expressed in official Israeli briefings to the foreign press.

Indeed, at this stage the Syrian threat was the main issue discussed between Israeli and American officials. The Israelis stressed that Syria was trying to derail the stability of the entire Middle East by both political and military means. Israeli spokesmen alleged that Syria wanted to forcibly change the region's political status quo that had been in effect since the War of 1948, by bringing a new player into the political arena – the Palestinian National Liberation Movement. Israel claimed that this trend could upset the delicate balance of power in the region that had been based exclusively, until now, on relations between sovereign states.[63]

The Israelis undoubtedly wanted to highlight the growing danger to the kingdom of Jordan, as well as to other pro-Western states in the region, that the Palestinians' strengthening and the rapidly developing ties between their leadership and the Syrian leaders portended. Eshkol naturally hoped that the White House would internalize his unsubtle message that the Syrian threat, and the Egyptian one that was looming in its shadow, had an impact not only on Israel but also on America's vital interests in the region.[64]

The Syrian menace also played a dominant role in the talks held between Foreign Minister Eban and Ambassador Barbour when the president's message was received. Eban discussed Syria's responsibility for initiating the crisis, referring to Egypt as the innocent bystander of Syria's scheming. Syria had also embroiled Jordan and Lebanon in the cauldron of hostility against Israel, who was well aware of Syria's cunning behavior. Israel's target was now Syria (not as in the case of the Samu operation); Israel appreciated the president's advice to act with restraint but wanted to know what the president suggested they do in the event of another Syrian-directed terrorist act. In that case, the US would certainly agree, Israeli restraint would no longer be justified.[65]

The United States' messages to Israel seemed to have implied that the Johnson administration suspected that the IDF was carrying out an independent Syrian policy, instigating the border tension without supplying all the details to the political level. Eban vehemently refuted these suspicions, stressing that the political level was fully in control of the army and the IDF had "no automatic switches open". Notwithstanding these unambiguous words, it is difficult to say whether Eban himself believed that what he was saying was reflecting the real situation "on the ground".[66]

Furthermore, when Eshkol met with Israeli newspaper editors on May 18, 1967, he focused on the Syrian theater, telling the editors that despite the IDF's proven superiority – especially that of the air force after the April 7 incident on the Golan Heights – Syria continued to channel hostile infiltration into Israel. This meant that the drubbing Syria incurred on April 7 had not created a sufficient degree of deterrence. In this light, it is surprising that Eshkol found it suitable to publicly warn Syria that if it pursued its hostile activity Israel would retaliate seven-fold. Did Eshkol really believe that such overstated bombast would obtain what had not been gained by military acts on the ground? The Syrians were spreading false rumors, Eshkol asserted, that Israel had concentrated massive fire-power on the northern border in preparation for an attack. Israel had accepted the proposal of the UN commander in the region, General Odd Bull, to allow the UN to verify Syria's charges. As of today, however, no answer had been received from Syria.[67]

Eshkol further conveyed details of the Egyptian layout in Sinai. According to the IDF's estimates, the Egyptian deployment was defensive in nature, primarily designed to threaten Israel so that it would not dare attack Syria. Despite these "reassurances", Eshkol also admitted that Israel had called up forces that it believed essential to ward off an Egyptian attack.[68]

6

Dramatic Change in the Perception of the Threat
The End of Exhibiting Restraint

Already at this stage one can discern in Eshkol's words a growing doubt over the credibility of the IDF's reassurances regarding the nature and intentions of the Egyptian activity. At a press conference Eshkol held with the editors of Israeli newspapers, Dr. Herzl Rosenblum – editor of the daily *Yediot Achronot* – asked him why the government persisted in feeding the press with calming reports and evaluations about Egyptian troop concentrations in Sinai. Eshkol admitted that these had been the dominant assessments at the beginning of the crisis, but that when Israeli officials meet with foreign diplomats "we scream bloody murder [over the Egyptian threat], but perhaps this is not enough". At this stage Eshkol was unwilling to say bluntly that the Soviet Union was behind the Egyptian moves. He did, however, imply that perhaps the Soviet leadership wished to "throw a firecracker", as he termed it, into the Middle East, probably in order to create some sort of "low-profile tension".[1]

On the evening of May 18, 1967, and even more so the following day, there were indications of a dramatic change in Israel's estimate of the crisis, as it was obvious that the fear of a descent to war had grown exponentially. In a meeting with Eugene Rostow on May 18, 1967, the Israeli ambassador to the United States, Avraham Harman, informed him that Israel was reassessing the situation. Though it still regarded the entry of the Egyptian army into Sinai as only for show, another situation estimate was in the process of being formulated, and errors in the accuracy of the first situation estimate have already been noted.[2]

At a meeting between Eban, the chief of Israeli intelligence, Aaron Yariv, and Ambassador Barbour on May 18, 1967, the two

Israelis stressed the turnabout in Israel's assessment of Egyptian military activity in Sinai, and the increasing anxiety over it. Indeed, the bulk of the conversation was devoted to a review of the Egyptian deployment and its threatening nature. Yariv stated that according to Israeli sources, seventy thousand Egyptian soldiers were currently amassed in Sinai – some of them only twenty kilometers from the border. Egypt had already brought in six hundred tanks. Replying to the ambassador's question about Egypt's solidarity with Syria, Eban gave a non-committal answer, estimating that Israel did not think that Egypt was planning to bring events to a confrontation: "[Israel] has not pushed the panic button [yet]."[3]

Eban also advised the Americans not to read too deeply into Egypt's basic motives in initiating the crisis, stressing that these motives were not necessarily relevant to the development of the crisis. Regardless of its main objectives, he asserted correctly, events have their own dynamics and developments are liable to be completely different from those that were expected or considered earlier. Israel would do everything in its power to avoid escalating the tension; nevertheless, it had to prepare itself for the worst case scenario.[4]

Eban concluded by reiterating the point that Eshkol had also raised in his letter to the president: the key to the peaceful solution of the crisis was in the Soviet's hands. Moscow alone could restrain Egypt and Syria. The most important thing the United States could do at this stage was to make it clear to the Soviet Union that the tension in the region could spin out of control, with devastating consequences. The best way to prevent this was by informing the Kremlin that it was not the only superpower with interests and involvement in the Middle East. This task, of course, was left to the US administration.[5]

On the same day, Rostow met with the Soviet consul in Washington to learn whether there was truth to the rumors circulating in the Syrian capital about a Soviet promise of unlimited military and political support. The Soviet representative stated that the rumors contradicted his country's official policy, "causing us serious damage". He declared that the Soviet Union was interested in creating a peaceful atmosphere in the Middle East. Rostow said that he had no doubt that the rumors were false. Still, it was important that the Soviet regime were aware of the grave consequences they could face if, in the minds of the Syrian and Egyptian leadership, this was the real assessment of Soviet commitments. Rostow made no demand or request from the Soviet diplomat – such as a public declaration by a high-ranking official regarding the Soviet Union's intentions. He may have avoided doing this because his partner in the conversation was a low-level diplomat, and his guarantees would, in any case, be of little value.[6]

The same day Rostow also met with Harman. The latter made it clear, this time more determinedly than in the past, that the Israeli government was intensely reevaluating the nature of Egypt's moves and the intentions which might stand behind it. Harman stressed that in view of the growing turnabout in the situation estimate, Israel had to take precautionary steps. Unlike its position of a few days earlier, Israel did not recoil from explicitly demanding that the administration "do something" to keep the UN force in Sinai and the Gaza Strip. At the same time Israel was undoubtedly aware that such a petition would be interpreted by the United States, as well as by neighboring Arab states, as expressing a lack of confidence and weakness.[7]

Israel also wanted Washington to realize the implications of Egypt's moves in Sinai regarding Syria. Israel, on its part, was convinced that the Egyptian moves would encourage Syria to undertake even more of a militant policy towards Israel. Israel also urged the US administration to formulate a lucid assessment regarding Moscow's role in the crisis, so that it could demand the Soviet Union to use its influence to restore calm to the region. Rostow made no reply to this request, only expressing his hope that the information about Egyptian forces having taken control of Sharm el-Sheikh was mistaken. Nevertheless, he must have been fully cognizant of the ramifications of such a serious escalation. This is why he reemphasized – although this time in softer, non-threatening language – that even if the data were accurate, it would be an error on Israel's part to initiate a military operation. This seems to have been one of the first signs of the growing *volte-face* in the Johnson administration's position on an Israeli-initiated strike against Egypt.[8]

On May 18, 1967, the Israeli government convened to discuss the developing crisis. The foreign ministry's deputy director for American affairs, Moshe Bitan, took part and reported on it afterwards to Ambassador Barbour. Bitan's report shows that a dramatic turnaround was taking place in Israel's assessment. Israel's main concern, as reflected in the government meeting, was Egypt's air power in Sinai, where it had concentrated 75–90 fighter aircraft. Bitan told the ambassador that Israel was extremely worried about the vulnerability of the nuclear reactor in Dimona.[9]

On the previous day, two Egyptian Mig 21s had crossed the Egyptian–Israeli border and flown over the reactor. Before the Israeli air force could scramble to pursue them, they disappeared into Sinai, causing the Israeli leadership to lose a considerable amount of sleep, and heightening their apprehension over Egyptian intentions to bomb the reactor. Bitan also informed Barbour that the government had decided not to take any military steps at this stage beyond calling up the reserves to reinforce the defense layout.[10]

The report reveals the degree of anxiety felt by the Israeli government over a possible Egyptian air attack on the reactor. One of the southern command's divisions was ordered to make preparations for repulsing a ground assault on the Dimona reactor. A few days after the May 18, 1967 meeting, Eshkol again expressed his fear of an Egyptian attempt to destroy the reactor: "I view Egyptian military activity with the utmost gravity," he told the ministerial committee for security on May 21, 1967. "In my opinion, the Egyptians will try to block Israeli shipping in the Straits of Tiran and bomb the Dimona reactor, and then follow up with an all-out attack on Israel."[11]

Discussions at GHQ on May 19, 1967, noted that the Egyptian force in Sinai numbered six hundred tanks. In a briefing at the GHQ forum, Yariv stated that "Egypt's latest moves have been a radical departure from the line it has pursued until now". He also pointed out that as long as pan-Arab cooperation was still only theoretical and the Egyptian order of battle relatively limited, "it is difficult to assume that the Egyptians have withdrawn from their basic assessment that the time is not ripe for dealing with Israel. Nevertheless, the latest moves at least testify to Egypt's inclination to take giant steps toward a confrontation and perhaps even initiate a clash of arms."[12]

When Yariv met with military attachés on May 19, 1967, it was obvious that the previous assessments regarding Egypt's intentions were no longer valid. The Israeli intelligence chief announced that the previous day a volte-face had occurred in Israel's military–political assessment. He divulged that the main problem now was Egypt, not Syria. Until recently Israeli intelligence had believed that Egypt was disinclined to go to war, however over the past few days Israel's situation assessment had changed. The

Soviet Union supported Egypt's military activity. In his opinion, Jordan would enter the fray only if it felt that Israel was on the verge of defeat, an assessment that would soon prove unsubstantiated and would become another of Israel's intelligence failures of the Six Day War, swept under the rug in the postwar victory euphoria felt by large segments of Israeli society. In any case, the American attaché reported that Yariv had demonstrated a lower level of self-confidence than usual, which was unsurprising.[13]

The dramatic turning-point in Israel's assessment of the threat it faced added to the heightened tension in Israel. The national leadership suddenly realized it was facing a political-military threat of a type it had not encountered since the War of 1948. When General Rhikye announced that the UN headquarters in Sinai no longer existed, Israeli leaders finally understood that the buffer was gone between its army and the Egyptian forces deployed in eastern Sinai. The strategic threat facing Israel in Sinai suddenly overshadowed the daily security threat posed by Syria and the Palestinian organizations.

Israel received no respite in the political arena either. To its dismay, it realized that its main ally, the United States, had essentially repudiated its commitments to guarantee Israel's security and maritime rights through the Straits of Tiran, and was even attempting to hamper Israel's freedom of military action. During a discussion in GHQ on May 19, 1967, the Chief-of-Staff gave sharp and incisive expression to Israel's acute isolation: "We have no one to rely on but ourselves. Anyone who expects someone else [to come to our aid] – will find himself badly mistaken."[14]

Last but not least, the crisis produced another change: a crack had been created in the credibility and effectiveness of Israel's military assessment in general, and the intelligence services in particular. The Chief-of-Staff Rabin, who was supposed to radiate confidence in the IDF in one of Israel's most crucial hours, fell into a "funk". Some members of the state's leadership saw that the longstanding belief in the intelligence community's ability to furnish a warning and accurate data in real time was unfounded and grossly over-exaggerated. One after the other, the intelligence estimates broke down, either partially or proved completely wrong. Thus, Levy Eshkol, who for years had been stigmatized as a weak and fawning personality, was catapulted by a twist of fate to the pinnacle of leadership during a period when the country's survival was at stake.[15]

Under these circumstances, it is not surprising that Ambassador

Barbour, who was privy to the various levels of Israeli clarifications and close to the state's leaders, reported to the State Department on May 19, 1967, that Israel had undergone a seismic *volte-face* in its crisis assessment. One of the key expressions of this reorientation was the insistent request that the United States reaffirm its commitments to Israel's security and territorial integrity. At this stage, after the UN had evacuated the Sharm el-Sheikh region and Egyptian forces were massively deployed to Sinai, Israel had to consider the very real possibility that Egypt would continue to escalate the crisis by blocking the Straits of Tiran to Israeli shipping.

Such a move would be an intolerable blow to Israel's deterrent image (which had already suffered a major setback by the ouster of the UNEF and entry of Egyptian forces). Under these vexing conditions, Israel soon discovered additional erosion in the Johnson administration's position towards it and the degree of freedom of action Washington was willing to grant her. With the impending threat of the Straits' closure, the Johnson administration explained to Israel that blocking of the Straits did not give it the right to an immediate response. The White House still expected Israel to consult with it about the steps it intended to take.[16]

In this state of affairs, Israel sought to discover what the United States really planned to do regarding freedom of navigation to and from the port of Eilat. An Israeli representative proposed that an American warship, currently located in the Gulf of Akaba, exit the Straits into the Indian Ocean, make a u-turn, and head back to Eilat – via the Straits. In this way the US could demonstrate its resolve to guarantee freedom of navigation in line with the commitments it made after the Sinai Campaign.

Although the plan undoubtedly had some positive factors, one cannot help wondering what the proposal was actually supposed to achieve. Egypt, at any rate, had not mentioned a word about blocking the Straits to American warships. The closure that the Israelis feared, and that eventually did happen, referred only to vessels flying the Israeli flag or to foreign ships carrying "strategic material" to Israel. An American warship was not included in either category, therefore the passage of a United States navy destroyer would achieve no practical purpose. Moreover, this would be a once-only voyage, and even if it succeeded there was no guarantee that other vessels would enjoy the same freedom. Simultaneously, Israel asked the United States to declare its willingness to provide it with military and economic aid, a request to which the administration responded negatively. Certain circles in the government announced that taking sides was likely to increase suspicion in the Arab world that the US was supporting Israel in the crisis.[17]

In addition, the Israeli government appealed to the United States to urgently send twenty thousand gas masks, following information that some of the Egyptian troops in Sinai were equipped with gas masks. Given the mounting tension in Israel during this period, it was only natural that rumors spread that Egypt was preparing to use chemical weapons as it had done in Yemen. At GHQ, on May 19, 1967, Rabin gave blatant expression to these fears: "If the Egyptians decide to go all out, they have a small amount of gas that they might use. I'm not in favor of circulating this information, but we have to realize that we lack protection . . . There is only one detection center [for chemical material] and it's deployed with the air force."[18]

Even if the probability of Egypt resorting to the chemical option was low, Israel was certainly justified in regarding it as a major issue. The unavoidable link between German scientists with Nazi résumés, who wanted to develop an unconventional weapons capability for Egypt, and the Nazis use of gas in the holocaust, was able to significantly strengthen Israel's apprehensions at this critical hour. At the same time these unique circumstances also enhanced Israel's political–moral standing. In view of the request for gas masks, Washington's crisis analysts were asked to update the government on the scope of Egypt's use of gas in Yemen. Parallel to this, the Johnson administration sent urgent economic aid to Israel.[19]

Israel's requests reflect the enormity of the country's concern over Egypt's military–political moves in the latter half of May. Against this background, as stated, a dramatic *volte-face* had taken place in the White House's perception of the crisis. Israel's distress signals were finally picked up by the Americans whose prognostications now became even more cataclysmic than those in Israel. On May 20, Rostow handed Secretary of State Rusk an apocalyptic situation assessment of Egypt's intentions. According to Rostow, the accepted assessment until now had been that the Egyptians were employing a "you'd better restrain me" tactic, but until now they had only been bluffing.[20]

Rostow added that he now questioned the validity of this evaluation, as one could not rule out the possibility that the Egyptians were preparing an attack on Israel using, *inter alia*, poison gas. The under-secretary recalled the report Israel had communicated to the administration stating that some of the Egyptian troops in Sinai had been supplied with gas masks, and therefore requested the immediate shipment of twenty thousand gas masks. The main question on the agenda, he concluded, was whether Egypt was about to launch a blitzkrieg, with or without coordination with the Soviets, while using massive doses of poison gas.[21]

On May 21, in light of a major setback in American support of Israel and the approaching danger of Egypt's closure of the Straits of Tiran to Israeli shipping, Eban asked to meet with Ambassador Barbour. The conversation took place after the Israeli government had held a lengthy, tension-filled meeting. Eban opened the conversation by stating Israel's estimate that the scope of its troop concentration on the southern front was capable of handling the Egyptian menace. He also told the ambassador – the first time so directly – that Israel was disappointed with the White House's position on the crisis, since the administration's identification with, and support of Israel was far below the level that his government had hoped to receive. Israel eagerly awaited the president's reply to Eshkol's letter of May 18.[22]

Eban asserted that the administration's reluctance to publicly reaffirm its commitments to Israel at this trying hour weighed heavily on the Jewish people, and could have grave effects. The foreign minister did not elaborate, probably wishing to signal to the White House that in the absence of American backing, Israeli public opinion might demand that the government act independently. In concrete terms, Israel expected Johnson to unequivocally restate his obligation to safeguard Israel's sovereignty, and reemphasize confidently the US obligation to guarantee navigational freedom through the Straits. Eban repeated Israel's disappointment at the Johnson administration's unwillingness – as opposed to the British and French positions – to supply Israel with weapons by claiming that the timing was unsuitable.[23]

During the conversation Eban raised several points of extreme importance for understanding Israel's views. According to Eban, Egypt had been planning the crisis for some time, proved by its troop reduction in Yemen before the eruption of the crisis. Freedom of navigation in the Straits was in Israel's supreme national interest. A decade ago, Eban recalled, the question of shipping in the Straits of Tiran was a problem of a legal nature, but today it was of vital national importance. Eban did not elaborate, but his meaning became clear as the conversation progressed; he was referring to the fact that nearly all of Israel's oil imports arrived from Iran via the Straits to the port of Eilat.[24]

Barbour did not try to refute this claim, and Washington was well aware of the economic importance of the Straits and Eilat. A State Department memo noted that the lion's share of Israel's oil came through the Straits of Tiran. Over three million tons of crude oil arrived in Eilat annually, before being transferred to refineries in Haifa. The only alternative was to transport oil around the Cape of Good Hope to the port of Haifa, a move that would increase the price of oil by approximately 30 percent. Excluding oil, other imports and exports valued at sixty million dollars a year passed through the port of Eilat, approximately 4 percent of Israel's imports and 7 percent of its exports. Beyond commercial considerations, the memo raised a point that had somehow been overlooked by Israeli officials: Eilat also bore a symbolic meaning that was linked, *inter alia*, to the city's reference in the Bible.[25]

Eban assured his listener that Israel had no interest in exacerbating the tension, instead preferring to lower its profile as much as possible. He told the ambassador that he had personally asked Israel's newspaper editors to refrain from referring to the Straits, lest the Israeli press provoke Egypt or put it in a position that might compel it to block the Straits in order to maintain its prestige in the Arab world. Eban also said that in the wake of the government meeting he could honestly say that Israel had no intention of launching a military operation. He did not limit this commitment to a time frame, but we may assume that he was only referring to the immediate future. Whatever the case, it is unclear why Eban thought it necessary to convey such a message to the administration. Undoubtedly such a guarantee would significantly narrow Israel's freedom to maneuver in the crisis, while pacifying Washington's concern about solving the crisis as soon as possible in a way that accommodated Israel's interests.[26]

As the conversation approached its conclusion, Eban found it fitting, for whatever reason, to discreetly inform the ambassador that the crisis "had imposed" strains on the Israeli leadership. He then went on and informed the ambassador that for several days the Chief-of-Staff Yitzhak Rabin had been in a daze. Eban did not elaborate on the nature of Rabin's "sickness". It was unclear whether the term he used was of a medical nature. It is indeed very difficult to understand what benefits Eban thought to gain from such an exposure of Israeli fears.[27]

Finally Eban raised the possibility of placing UN forces at "strategic points" such as Sharm el-Sheikh. While it was true, Eban claimed, that these forces had been evacuated from Sinai, they were still in the region and could be redeployed at several sensitive junctions. Eban probably broached this idea in the hope that the administration would sell it to the Secretary-General, who would then present it to the Egyptians. But the very suggestion of the idea underscored the effect that Egypt's moves had on the Israeli leadership's nerves and shattered confidence. The essence of the proposal was that UN troops should be relied on to deter Nasser from blocking the Straits of Tiran. In this light, Israel's status as a deterrent power was eroding since it was willing to downsize its status in order to avoid a full-scale military confrontation.[28]

Barbour responded to Eban's criticism of American policy by claiming that the US was refraining from public declarations of support for Israel due to tactical purposes. Washington was being accused of plotting with Israel against the Arab world. As for the current crisis, the Arab world believed that the Johnson administration backed Israel. Statements by American figures regarding freedom of navigation in the Straits were perceived by Arabs – especially in Egypt – as an indication of an anti-Arab position. Thus, any additional broadcasting of support would aggravate the United States' position even more, making it extremely difficult for Washington to preserve an objective image that would assist in a peaceful solution to the crisis.[29]

The ambassador reported his lengthy conversation with Eban to the heads of the administration, noting that: (a) at the present time, as long as Egypt has not decided to block the Straits, Israel will not initiate direct military action; (b) Israel will do everything in its power, regardless of the risks entailed, to open the Straits of Tiran in the event that Egypt closes them to Israeli shipping; and (c) Israel believes that the United States is obligated to assist it on the basis of its 1957 commitment to guarantee Israeli passage through the Straits, and on the basis of other commitments.[30]

In its efforts to resolve the crisis, the Johnson administration attempted to get through to leaders in Damascus. In a meeting between the United States ambassador to Syria and the Syrian Foreign Minister, Ibrahim Machus, on May 20, the American made a valiant attempt to convince his listener to lower his country's rhetoric so that an atmosphere would be created conducive to a peaceful resolution of the crisis. The ambassador soon realized that his efforts were futile. Encouraged by Egypt's full backing and the openly declared support of the Soviet Union, and awareness of the anxiety and uncertainty in Israel, Syria saw no need to make any kind of token gesture toward a settlement.[31]

Under these circumstances, the radicalization of Syria's position on the crisis and its settlement came to flagrant expression. Machus repeated the charge that Israel harbored aggressive intentions, also stating that the Palestinian issue was "sacred" and would never be forgotten until the dreams of the Palestinian people were realized. According to the Syrian Foreign Minister, Palestinian terrorism was completely justified; no one had the right to deny them their struggle for freedom. They had been waiting eighteen years for the UN to solve their problem, he said, and nothing had come of it. Israel's very existence was the epitome of aggression. Machus went back to the crusader period for proof that no conquest was permanent, warning that the Arab world, beaming with self-confidence, was prepared for war. Any Israeli provocation would ignite the fuse.[32]

On May 21, Eban sent an urgent message to the Secretary-General, expressing Israel's fears if the Straits were blocked. The message stressed that the Israeli government regarded freedom of navigation through the Straits of Tiran to be of supreme national interest, and that it would defend this right at any cost. Israel would not agree to return to the situation that prevailed prior to the Sinai Campaign when the Straits were closed to Israeli vessels. This position was also brought to the attention of other governments that supported maritime freedom.[33]

Eban justifiably avoided direct criticism of the Secretary-General over his decision to evacuate the UN troops, as it would only alienate U Thant further. With war looming on the horizon, Israel was likely to need his good will at one stage or another. Israel thus wisely chose to accuse the machinery that enabled such a decision to be made without taking steps to guarantee freedom of navigation, rather than the secretary general himself. Eban concluded his message by pointing out that Israel had avoided giving publicity to the freedom of navigation issue in order to facilitate the political efforts in resolving the crisis.[34]

On the same day, Johnson sent another message to the prime minister, repeating his understanding of Israel's difficult situation. The president also agreed that in order to restore calm to the region

Arab terrorism had to end, and the military steps Egypt took had to be redressed. The administration was doing everything in its power to clarify its position to the Egyptian and Syrian governments. Simultaneously he reiterated his demand that Israel gird itself with nerves of steel and exhibit restraint so as not to further deteriorate the situation.[35]

Johnson congratulated Eshkol for bringing to his attention the fact that Israel's military measures were only a precautionary and defensive nature. This implied a US understanding that Israel was not contemplating launching a military offensive in the future. Any change in the posture of the Israeli army deployment could therefore be interpreted as a breach of that Israeli undertaking.[36]

The president's message avoided reference to the American obligation to guarantee Israel's sovereignty in the event of aggressive threats against it. Johnson also urged Israel to consider stationing UN forces on its soil, an idea that the administration had broached on a number of occasions but that Israel had firmly rejected. The president also mentioned – undoubtedly in response to Israeli insistent behest – that the United States was in constant communication with the Soviet leadership, urging it to restrain Egypt and Syria. Johnson was convinced that the Kremlin was aware of the American position on the crisis. Furthermore, the Soviet Union's responses to his messages were encouraging, demonstrating a realization in Moscow that Washington was determined to avert aggressive conduct in the Middle East.[37]

The next day Johnson sent a message to Nasser, written in blandishing, almost sycophantic language. Johnson appeared to have made every effort to make Nasser feel that Egypt and the United States had no reason to be in a state of conflict, since both countries were striving for identical goals. Nevertheless, the message could not conceal a bluntly critical view of Egypt's recent belligerent moves, and the dangers they held for the national interests of the Arab world, particularly Egypt.[38]

The president began his message by stating that he had devoted a great deal of attention to the Mideast crisis, and the problems that "you" and "we" are facing. He then attempted to flatter Nasser, acknowledging that he had been following the Egyptian president's efforts to bring his nation into the modern age. He also hinted that his administration was willing to extend economic assistance to Egypt through both direct aid and private means. Johnson expressed his understanding of the pressures under which

Nasser was working in the pan-Arab arena, which may have forced him, so the president implied, to radicalize his policy toward Israel.[39]

The American president displayed sensitivity to certain "time-honored memories" (the reference was probably to the creation of the Palestinian refugee problem after the Arab defeat in the 1948 war and the three-pronged attack on Egypt by Israel, Britain, and France in the Sinai Campaign). Johnson tried to create a common link with Nasser by emphasizing that "your" role and "mine" is not to look back but to look forward. We must do everything to save the Middle East and the entire international system from a war that nobody wants.[40]

Johnson's "buttering up" was evidently designed to soften Nasser's response to the criticism – which was necessary but still mild at this stage – of Egypt's warlike steps. He avowed that the great conflicts in our time would not be solved by crossing borders and stockpiling weapons – not in Asia (Vietnam) or anywhere else (the Middle East). Thus, quietly and discreetly Johnson compared North Vietnam's aggression against the United States to Egypt's belligerent activity against Israel. In the heated atmosphere of this period, when North Vietnam was depicted as an "axis of evil" supported by world communism, the American president could not have reproached Egypt in stronger terms.[41]

The message of President Johnson to Nasser thus contained a subtle warning: Egypt had better take into account the possibility that, just as the United States was backing South Vietnam, it might also take sides with Israel against Egypt, although not necessarily with the same equipment and means. In conclusion Johnson informed Nasser that despite the differences between their countries, Egypt and the United States both shared a common goal – Egypt's economic prosperity and growth. These words certainly implied that if Egypt would show tendency towards a peaceful solution to the crisis, the United States would be willing to provide her with generous economic support. Johnson also expressed his belief that Nasser, as the leader of the Arab world, would act in his people's interests, refraining from provocations that could spark a conflagration in the region. Johnson then disclosed that he was considering sending Vice President Humphrey to the region to handle negotiations for resolving the crisis. A similar message was communicated to the Syrian president.[42]

The president's message – despite its compromising and somewhat adulating style – undoubtedly expressed the changes in Johnson's position on the crisis. The administration seems to have started to realize that a policy which completely ignored the serious threat facing Israel, and which forbade Israel even minimal freedom of action would not result in a calming of the situation, but the opposite: it would encourage Nasser to escalate the crisis, thus goading Israel into launching a preemptive strike. We may assume that the White House formulated a more balanced position that would at least restrain Egypt's "*idée fixe*" to block the Straits of Tiran to Israeli shipping.

The US soon realized that its threats, like those of Israel – whether overt or concealed – were not a deterrent factor as far as Nasser was concerned. Johnson's message failed to mitigate Egypt's aggressive tendencies and militant maneuverings, leading the Johnson administration to realize that Egypt was liable to close the Straits of Tiran in the very near future. Fearing the worst, Rostow invited Egypt's ambassador to the United States, Mustafa Kamel, for talks aimed at convincing Egypt not to cross the Rubicon by taking a step that Israel perceived as a declaration of war or, as Rostow described it, contained "grave consequences". The American under-secretary emphasized that such a move would severely imperil Israel's vital interests.[43]

The White House's understanding of Israel's vital interests undoubtedly referred to the import of oil from Iran. According to American estimates, Israel imported four million tons of oil per year (95 percent of which arrived through Eilat). Half of the oil was used for domestic needs, and the rest was transferred to refineries in Haifa before being sold in Europe through an American company. Against this background, Washington figured that the closing of the Straits would deal a heavy economic blow to Israel in addition to the grievous political-security damage involved in such a step. For this reason, the US State Department memo declared that the blockade of the Straits was a flagrant violation of international law, and an act of aggression.[44]

On May 22, 1967, the American ambassador to Egypt received instructions to set up an urgent meeting with Egyptian Foreign Minister Mahmud Riad and convey Washington's positions in the clearest terms. There could be no doubt now that Washington had formulated a coherent position on the crisis and its causes. Nevertheless, the ambassador's instructions were prudently stated so as not to push Egypt into the corner and incite it to further escalation. The administration presented Egypt and Israel as two countries that were liable to stumble into a head-on collision that neither wanted. At present, both states were highly suspicious of one another, therefore in such an explosive condition a rash move could ignite a regional conflagration. Egypt and Israel had to understand that war harbored grave dangers not only for the Middle East and their respective countries, but for the entire world.[45]

The two contending sides had to stop in their tracks and realize that they had come to this unfortunate situation because of warmongering activity of a third party – Syria. Syrian-instigated terror, the administration averred, was opposed to the Armistice Agreements, a fact that Egypt had to recognize. Next, a supreme effort would have to be made to restore the situation to its previous state, though the ouster of the UNEF hampered a solution to the crisis. The reinforcement of troops by the two sides – albeit for defensive purposes only, according to their admissions – made it very difficult to pursue quiet diplomacy.[46]

Finally, the most important step Egypt and Israel could do at present was to pull their forces back to their original positions, and if possible, have the UNEF remain in or return to Sinai. The worst mistake would be to strain tensions even more by blocking the Straits of Tiran to Israeli vessels. However, in light of Egypt's refusal to heed the appeals and warnings, the United States had to call attention to its commitment to maritime freedom in the Straits of Tiran, which was of vital interest not only to Israel but to the international community. Any infringement of this principle would have severe ramifications on the entire international system.[47]

These instructions must have symbolized a major turning point in Washington's position on the crisis. The Johnson administration apparently concluded that Egypt's activity was an egregious provocation, not only to Israel but also to the United States and its interests in the region. The White House undoubtedly believed that Egypt had coordinated with America's key rival in the international theater – the Soviet Union. To the best of our knowledge, American policymakers realized that "sweet talk" and quiet diplomacy would fail to deflect Egypt from racing headlong toward a showdown with Israel at this stage. Under these circumstances, Egypt had to be told the following "facts of life" in stiff and blunt language:

1. The administration regards the closure of the Straits as an aggressive act. This might imply that a military counter-

response by Israel is likely to be supported by the administration.

2. The Egyptian regime must understand that the United States stands behind its commitments to Israel. The meaning is clear: aggressive action against Israel holds the potential of an Egyptian–American confrontation.

3. Egypt should not delude itself by thinking it can make significant gains by attacking Israel. In all circumstances the US will endeavor to terminate the combat as quickly as possible, even if one side succeeds in attaining a significant military advantage.

On May 22, Prime Minister Eshkol made a political announcement in the Knesset, basically restating the above-mentioned American communiqués. Eshkol proposed that Israel and Egypt jointly limit their troop concentrations on the southern front, calling for an international effort to declare terrorism and sabotage against a UN member state illegal. He expressed hope that a long period of quiet like that which had prevailed on the Israeli–Egyptian border for years would resume. He also pointed to Syrian hostility against Israel as the factor directly responsible for the rise in regional tension.[48]

For a long time Israel had exhibited restraint before responding, until it had been forced to take measures to guarantee its security. The Prime Minister condemned the evacuation of the UN troops from Sinai, claiming it had weakened the UN's status as the world's peace-preserving organization. He charged that the Secretary-General had acted against the promises that his predecessor, Dag Hammarskjöld, had given Israel regarding the Secretary-General's obligation to consult with a number of states before removing UN forces from Sinai.[49]

7

Blocking the Straits of Tiran
The US Regards Egyptian Moves as Provocation

In the early hours of the morning on May 23, President Nasser's decision to close the Straits of Tiran to Israeli shipping became known following his declaration in a speech to Egyptian officers in Sinai the previous day. His statements, as expected, had been uttered in a boastful, provocative tone, promising that under no circumstances would he allow Israeli-flagged ships to pass through the Straits. He called on Islamic states (a broad hint to Iran) to contribute to the Palestinian issue and prevent the flow of oil to Israel, mocking Israel's threats of war: "If it's war that it wants, then *ahlan wa'sahlan* [welcome] war it will get."[1]

The timing of his decision was undoubtedly heavily influenced by U Thant's decision to travel to Egypt for talks on resolving the crisis. Egypt had to present the Secretary-General with a *fait accompli* before he landed in the region. From the American perspective, Egypt's decision was a ringing slap in the face that made mockery of President Johnson's threats. The Israelis viewed the closure of the Straits as a fatal decision, symbolizing the collapse of Israel's deterrence system vis-à-vis Egypt.[2]

In light of the dramatic heightening in the tension between Egypt and Israel, an immediate situation assessment was needed to clarify the implications of the Egyptian decision and Israel's likely reaction. The White House's initial estimate was that Israel's commitment to consult with it prior to any military action had been given because of the tension created by the UN evacuation from Sinai and entry of Egyptian troops. Now the circumstances had radically changed; Egypt had taken a definite step toward war, and the United States could only restrain Israel from responding with force over the next twenty-four hours.[3]

The American ambassador to the Soviet Union was instructed to persuade the Soviets to use their influence to convince Egypt to halt the downslide to war. The ambassador was asked to remind the Soviet Foreign Minister, Andrei Gromyko, that Russian leaders had repeatedly declared that no state in the region wanted a war. On the practical level the ambassador was authorized to divulge information to Gromyko – the contents of which is still unclear – that had generated concern in the administration.[4]

Indeed, the same day that the American ambassador received these instructions he met with Foreign Minister Gromyko. Speaking with the ambassador, Gromyko changed the part in the ambassador's text that said, "no state in the region wants war" to "war is not necessary to any state". Naturally, this sentence was intended to substantiate the Soviet "thesis" that distinguished between the Israeli government and its "aggressive interests" and the fundamentally peace-loving Israeli people. War, then, was unnecessary for any state in the region. The Soviets alleged that certain circles in Israel definitely sought a military confrontation since they believed that war would realize their interests and those of the Western superpowers that they serve.[5]

At the same time, Under-Secretary of State Eugene Rostow met with the Egyptian ambassador, Mustafa Kamel. Rostow remarked that the Egyptian government had to understand that the United States would make every effort to prevent war. Passage through the Straits was of vital interest to Israel and a legal right; their closure would be a blatant violation of international law, and an act of aggression from the administration's point of view. Rostow expressed his hope that Egypt would reconsider its decision, to which Kamel replied that the crisis could have been prevented had the US answered Egypt's earlier requests.[6]

Kamel wanted to create the impression that it was still possible to resolve the crisis without resorting to armed conflict. Under the present circumstances, he said, the UN Secretary-General had to be supported on his mission to Cairo. Kamel also proposed dispatching certain high-ranking American officials who were acceptable to the Arab states to Egypt, for example: Robert Anderson, Eugene Black, and John McCoy. The Egyptian diplomat asked the administration to soften its anti-Egypt media blitz, concluding by saying that the situation was still not out of control.[7]

On May 23, the new American ambassador to Egypt, Richard Nolte, held a meeting with Egyptian Foreign Minister Mahmud Riad. This was only Nolte's second day on the job, however he sounded confident and the messages he conveyed to the Egyptians left no room for doubt regarding the United States' position on the crisis. The ambassador recalled that four American presidents had committed the US to halting aggressive activity – open or covert – by any party in the Middle East, and safeguarding the sovereignty and territorial integrity of all states in the region. The White House hoped that the Egyptian government was aware of this. Nolte also made clear that Washington was making every effort to prevent war from erupting, and would broker a ceasefire if and when it broke out.[8]

Nolte confirmed that as part of the United States' efforts it was urging Israel to exercise maximum restraint. Even taking this into account, he stressed, freedom of navigation in the Straits had far-reaching implications, and the US viewed any infringement upon this principle as an act of aggression. Regarding the closure of the Straits of Tiran to Israeli vessels, Riad said that Egypt intended to detain Israeli ships and expropriate strategic cargos and foreign-flagged vessels bound for Israel. He guaranteed that his country would not carry out an offensive act, but would defend itself with determination against any attack. Despite his newness to the job, ambassador Nolte immediately realized that Egypt's actions were intended to hurt not only Israel but also the US, therefore in a memo to the State Department he declared that Egypt had put itself on a collision course with the United States.[9]

On the same day, Under-Secretary of State Rostow met with Israeli minister Ephraim Evron at the Israeli embassy in the United States. Rostow informed Evron that Israel's requests for military and economic aid were on President Johnson's desk, and that the president would probably decide on the matter shortly. Rostow's statement was undoubtedly intended to assuage Israel's anger over what it regarded as Washington's "lukewarm" policy in the crisis, and its reluctance to give public support for Israel's positions. He also wanted to encourage Israel to proceed with restraint, pressing home the fact that the economic ramifications of blocking the Straits of Tiran could be solved with American aid. Furthermore, Rostow claimed, the president had decided to shun public declarations on the crisis in order to deal with the crisis through quiet diplomacy.[10]

During the conversation Rostow repeated the demand that Israel "consult" with the administration before embarking upon a military response. The closure of the Straits, he stressed, had created an extremely dangerous situation in the region, therefore frequent consultation between Israel and the United States was needed now more than ever. The US, Rostow said, was convening an informal meeting of the Security Council, and hoped that a shooting incident would not occur prior to that. He was convinced that the debate on the Straits of Tiran should be postponed until it came up for discussion in the Security Council. Rostow mentioned his conversation with the Egyptian ambassador to Evron, who replied that the situation was not irreversible. Britain too, Rostow noted, had initiated moves that included additional "maritime states" in the effort to safeguard freedom of passage through the Straits.[11]

Rostow must have thought that Evron would be satisfied to hear that the British initiative was designed to include the Security Council in its solution to the crisis. Israel, however, justifiably felt that involvement of the Security Council would only create needless foot-dragging on the issue, during which Israel would be prevented from acting. The only outcome of this diplomatic flurry would be an unacceptable solution to both parties, and in the time interval Egypt would cement its hold on the Straits. The upshot would be that Israel's freedom of maneuvering would be significantly reduced, and its ability to restore the situation to its pre-crisis condition would be seriously impaired.[12]

As a result, Evron's response to the proposal was most reserved; he recalled that the Soviet Union had the right to cast a veto that could cut short the ratification of a decision opposed to the Egyptian position. Under these circumstances Rostow could only say to Evron – with admirable candor – that bringing the issue to the Security Council could serve as an important tactical step to justify an Israeli military operation against Egypt. If Israel did embark upon such a course, he stated, American public opinion would only accept it if it was preceded by serious efforts at finding a political solution.[13]

Rostow's statement seems to testify the Johnson administrations increasing realization that an Israeli military strike was inevitable if it wished to guarantee freedom of navigation through the Straits of Tiran and the removal of Egyptian divisions from Sinai. The White House was aware of the deep concern in Israel over an angry reaction by the administration if it initiated a military operation. Against this background, the United States' subtle message to Israel that it would not oppose an Israeli strike against Egypt was clearly perceived in Israel as an encouraging step.[14]

On May 23 Ambassador Harman met with former President Eisenhower. During Eisenhower's term of office, understandings had been reached relating to Israel's right to pass through the Straits, therefore it was imperative to obtain a token of support for Israel's position from the former president. Eisenhower justified Israel's position on passage through the Straits, but refused to issue a public announcement, only agreeing to state his opinion if asked. Harman perceived that Eisenhower had second thoughts on his conduct after the Sinai Campaign, when he had joined the Soviet Union in exerting massive pressure on Israel to withdraw almost unconditionally from the Sinai Peninsula. Johnson also asked Eisenhower to express public support for his (Johnson's) position on the crisis as they appeared in his May 23 public announcement. Eisenhower admitted that in 1957 the United States had promised Israel that if the Egyptians blocked transportation through the Straits, Israel would be allowed to act according to section 51 of the UN charter, that permits states to exercise their rights within the framework of the principle of self-defense.[15]

In addition to diplomatic contact with Israel and Egypt, the United States and Britain worked together to find solutions to the Mideast crisis. On May 23 the British Foreign Minister, George Brown, told the United States ambassador to Britain, David Bruce, that the British cabinet was about to discuss a proposal for the US, and other countries, to participate with Britain in a joint declaration underscoring the need to guarantee freedom of navigation through the Straits of Tiran. The proposal would have to include coordinated activity among the participating countries' navies.[16]

Washington eagerly took advantage of the ambassador's report, since it was convenient to have Britain leading the struggle for navigational freedom while the United States remained in the background providing support. In a meeting between the British ambassador to the United States, Sir Patrick Dean, and Under-Secretary of State, Rostow, the latter stated that the US welcomed the idea of formulating a declaration of intent and establishing a "multinational naval force" to protect freedom of navigation through the Straits. He emphasized that, for various reasons, the United States did not want to stand in the forefront of this struggle, preferring Britain to take the lead in initiating contact with countries such as Belgium, Holland, Canada, Japan, and Argentina.[17]

Rostow's attempt to kick the ball into Britain's court by saddling it with the primary responsibility for guaranteeing shipping freedom through the Straits does not seem to have been appreciated by the British ambassador. Sir Patrick preferred to see the United States shoulder the burden, with Britain lending full support from the background. Britain would happily participate in American-initiated activity, the ambassador promised, but he could not say whether his government wanted to stand in the front line of the struggle.[18]

Rostow stubbornly tried to convince Britain to agree to assume the lead in this task, offering to go "the extra mile" by pointing to America's willingness to participate in the initiative. Rostow told Sir Patrick that Britain could inform the countries that the proposal had American backing. Finally, the two parties realized that they were arguing over "an egg that hadn't even hatched yet", agreeing that steps must be taken to organize the multinational naval force without delay, but they were unable to decide who would lead the process.[19]

On May 23, a presidential statement was issued concerning the grave threat to peace overshadowing the Middle East crisis. The statement announced that the blocking of the Straits was illegal because the United States regarded the Straits of Tiran as an international maritime lane, vital to the international community. The American administration was deeply committed to safeguarding the political independence and territorial integrity of all the states in the region. Every American administration had sworn that it would repulse any form of aggression in the region – whether overt or subversive, a position maintained by the present administration. Israel could not have imagined a stronger declaration of intent from the Johnson administration. Nevertheless, the president's statement sharply limited Israel's maneuverability, as Israel was still denied the freedom to act unilaterally until it had exhausted all of the president's options into practical policy.[20]

To complicate matters, administration officials continued to send signals that somehow contradicted the president's messages. According to these signals, the White House would not interfere if Israel decided to act unilaterally to guarantee the freedom of its ships through the Straits. Despite this, the last thing the administration wanted now was to publicize its official recognition of Israel's shipping rights in the Red Sea. The Johnson administration wished Israeli representatives would understand Washington's dilemma between agreeing in principle to Israel's legal claims and the fear that overt identification with Israel's plight would irrevocably ruin America's relations in the Arab world, confirming Arab claims that the US supported Israel's aggressive plans. Under these circumstances, the Johnson administration hoped that Israel would take their situation into account and ease its pressure on the White House to define its positions.

As time passed, it was gradually realized that the British plan to establish a maritime taskforce was far from practical in the near future. In discussions held on May 24 between Under-Secretary of State Rostow and British minister of state for foreign affairs, George Thomson, it became clear that Britain had no interest in being depicted as the leading player in the plan. At the start of the conversation Thomson pointed out that the plan called for international agreement – not just a British–American understanding, and the two superpowers would have to operate within the framework of the UN. Also, every Western proposal dealing with the crisis could expect a Soviet veto. Administration officials, too, thought it preferable to secure the plan with broad international consent, stating that the administration's agreement to the plan required congressional support.[21]

To recall: the White House was still plagued by the "Gulf of Tonkin incident" in this period (the shelling of an American warship in the waters off South Vietnam). The president and other key administration figures were repeatedly accused – especially by congressmen – of misleading congress in 1964 when they asked for its agreement to use military force against North Vietnam after the Tonkin incident. Whatever the case, it was obvious that the stipulation of congressional approval paralyzed the chances of actualizing the British plan in the foreseeable future. Congressional agreement for such a risky venture would demand a relatively long effort from the Johnson administration. In practical terms this meant that the new status quo – the blockaded Straits – would remain in effect. The international system would increasingly adjust itself to the new situation and Israel's ability to rectify the situation would diminish.[22]

While this was happening, France continued its efforts to convince Britain and the US to transfer talks to a forum made up of all four superpowers. On May 24 the French ambassador to the United States, Charles Lucet, met with Rostow. During the meeting Lucet proposed convoking a discussion on the crisis with representatives of the four superpowers. The goal would be to make sure that none of the four parties acted in a way that could lead to a military confrontation between them. Rostow stated that the United States was interested in the meeting, but the Soviet Union was opposed to it. According to the under-secretary, the important thing was not the meeting itself, but the superpower's ability to reach a *modus vivendi*.[23]

Rostow also emphasized the growing realization in the administration that war was almost unavoidable, and that Washington's ability to stop Israel from launching a preemptive strike was exceedingly limited, and in any case would not be effective much longer. Rostow wanted to know if France's declarations, that required Israel and Egypt to avoid steps that could aggravate the situation, were not really a demand for Israel to refrain from taking action to lift the blockade on the Straits of Tiran. Rostow told Lucet that American pressure on Israel to not send a vessel through the Straits could not continue indefinitely. It was unrealistic to expect Israel to postpone a military operation much longer, unless it received Egyptian guarantees that the Straits would remain open. The main problem, Rostow stated forcefully, was that the principle of free movement through the Straits could not be compromised.[24]

Rostow's statements accurately reflect Washington's inflexible position toward Egypt at this stage. Nasser's decision to blockade the Straits of Tiran seemed to have been the straw that broke the camel's back. The Johnson administration was far from expressing outright support for the Israeli position and putting itself on a collision course with Egypt. Nevertheless, unlike its policy at the start of the crisis, it now seemed to regard Egyptian activity as a provocation aimed not only at Israel, but also at the United States. This is how Rostow's request of ambassador Lucet, that France refuse Egypt's appeal to sell it wheat should be seen. The present time is not right, Rostow told him, to appease Nasser.[25]

8

Abba Eban's Mission: Phase I
The Proposal for an International Naval Force

Under these extremely severe and exceptional circumstances, the government convened on May 23, 1967 to discuss matters of crucial importance for the fate of Israel, primarily the possibility of a military operation against Egypt. The IDF representatives, especially Generals Aharon Yariv and Ezer Weitzman, demanded immediate approval for a preventative strike. According to General Yariv, the chief of military intelligence, more than the question of maritime rights was involved in the provocative Egyptian moves. "If Israel doesn't respond to the closure of the Straits," he stressed, "then the IDF's credibility and deterrent power will no longer be worth much."[1]

General Weitzman, the head of GHQ and former commander of the air force, also called for an immediate air strike against Egypt. The Chief-of-Staff, Yitzhak Rabin, emphasized the severity of the threat posed on Israel, claiming that Israel was facing a war of survival, a position that reflected the dominant thinking within the government and the general public. However, unlike Yariv and Weitzman, during the government meeting Rabin was hesitant about supporting a belligerent move against Egypt. His emphasis on the dangers involved in an aerial strike created doubts in the minds of the Israeli leadership regarding its efficacy.[2]

Egypt's latest moves, which included the massive entry of forces into Sinai, the ouster of the UNEF from Sinai and the Gaza Strip, and the blocking of the Straits of Tiran to Israeli shipping, were obviously brazen provocations for Israel and the Western powers. They were interpreted by Israel as signifying the total collapse of its deterrent ability, dealing a serious blow to its economic strength and its strategic position in the regional and international arenas. From this point of view, an Israeli military strike seemed unavoidable. However, Israel had to be careful not to make a decision that ran counter to the demands of President Johnson to avoid undertaking unilateral steps without consulting the administration.

The dangers that Israel faced were clear; if it launched a strike against Egypt it risked involvement in a long and bloody military campaign during which it would crucially need US support. This American support was far from certain if Israel decided to undertake steps that were not considered beneficial to US interests. Furthermore, on the operational level, one could not ignore the possibility that Egypt was setting a trap for Israel to force it to respond immediately while Egypt was at the peak of operational alert.[3]

The government meeting lasted several hours. Washington was fully aware of the far-reaching implications of the decisions that might be made in this meeting. From the United States' perspective, its national interests at this stage required an effort to be made to avoid an Arab–Israeli confrontation. Against this background, Foreign Minister Eban informed his colleagues of the American message to Israel. The US recognized the seriousness of the situation, and was determined to honor American commitments (to guarantee freedom of shipping through the Straits of Tiran) by means of diplomatic activity inside and outside the UN. This route did not seem to lead to any satisfactory solution as far as Israel was concerned. However, on the agenda also stood the British proposal for establishing a naval task force to protect navigational freedom through the Straits.[4]

The plan was vague, with no specifications concerning how it would be realized or its time frame. Administration officials rightly reckoned that, bearing in mind the lack of acceptable and realistic alternatives, Israel would be satisfied at this stage by almost any display of Washington's willingness to take action to lift the blockade, even if the Israelis doubted the plan's practicality. Simultaneously, in order to make sure that Israel would not launch a military response, American officials, headed by Ambassador Barbour, reminded Israeli representatives of their country's promise to consult with the administration prior to any military action. More concretely, Israel was being asked not to decide on a response for the following forty-eight hours and to consult with the United States on the nature of the response.[5]

This British plan offered the Israeli government an easy way out of having to decide on a military strike against Egypt (which it was not yet ready to undertake), while not significantly forfeiting its prestige and deterrent strength. Israel could project the image that it was "keen" on responding forcibly to Egypt's provocations. It was prevented from doing so, however, by the pressure and demands of the superpowers, primarily the United States. In reality, most of the Israeli cabinet ministers still felt that a political solution to the crisis might be reached, and that war with Egypt could be prevented. Some of these "dovish" ministers opposed, almost on principle, the idea of an Israeli-initiated offensive, while other ministers did not reject a military strike per se, but recognized the need to exhaust the political tracks before taking the military "highroad".[6]

Even Yitzhak Rabin, the Chief-of-Staff, expressed an extremely cautious – almost apprehensive – position to the ministers regarding Israel's military response. In effect, he seemed to project the image that he was supporting the decision to continue seeking political means for ending the crisis. However, as the Chief-of-Staff, he had to demonstrate confidence in the IDF to solve the crisis by military means.[7]

In such a situation, when the person at the head of the military level suggests avoiding military action, the government ministers could easily decide to "proceed with the political activity". It must have been clear to the ministers that the absence of a decision for a military response – after [Israel] had repeatedly warned over the years that Egypt's closure of the Straits would be considered a *casus belli* – could only be interpreted as a capitulation to the Egyptian dictate. However, the American message and the Chief-of-Staff's position gave the Israeli government an outlet, even if only a temporary one, from the grave dilemma it was enmeshed in following Egypt's belligerent moves.

Israel wished to show that it rejected Washington's request "perfunctorily" and that it retained the military option. This option would be implemented if the administration's plan for establishing an international maritime force for protecting Israeli shipping through the Straits turned out to be impractical. Thus, the Israeli government decided to send Foreign Minister Abba Eban to Washington. Outwardly, Eban's mission could be presented as an expression of Israel's willingness to accept the White House's request to consult with it on the means of guaranteeing freedom of navigation without recourse to belligerency. However, "deep inside" the Israeli ministers had no illusions about the bitter and painful reality. Israel's situation was critical; it was faced with an extremely grave provocation without knowing how to respond, aware that its room for maneuvering was extremely limited.[8]

Eban's Meetings with French and British Leaders

Officially the government decision included three sections: (a) The government regards the closure of the Straits of Tiran to Israeli shipping as an act of aggression against Israel; (b) The government has decided to postpone the decision on its response to the closure of the Straits for forty-eight hours. During this time the Foreign Minister will learn the United States' position (with regard to the implementation of the plan); and (c) The government has decided to authorize the Prime Minister and Foreign Minister, if necessary, to decide on the Foreign Minister's journey to the United States for a meeting with the president of the US.[9]

As stated, the mission's aim was to examine the practicality of the British and American proposal to establish an international naval force that would guarantee maritime freedom through the Straits. The decision for Eban's mission was undoubtedly made in the awareness of the substantial dangers it portended for Israel's freedom of action in the crisis. At the conclusion of the meetings in Washington, Israel might find itself in a graver situation than before the mission, the new reality possibly including the following unfavorable scenarios:

1. The American administration would retain its policy that it stands by its commitments to Israel regarding ensuring her freedom of navigation through the Straits of Tiran, and her sovereignty and territorial integrity.
2. The administration would inform Israel that it opposed an Israeli-initiated military action despite Israel's critical situation, advising Israel to back the British–American plan notwithstanding the fact that its likelihood of realization in the foreseeable future was uncertain.

These clarifications would be given at the highest level of the American government – the presidential level – to a very high level in Israel (the Deputy Prime Minister/Foreign Minister). This meant that after the Eban–Johnson meetings, Israel's ability to maneuver among the different levels of the administration would be seriously curtailed.

Under these circumstances, Israel would face a painful dilemma in the process of formulating its response to the Egyptian moves. Israel could ignore the president's "recommendations" to avoid a military response in the near future. It would act independently, running the risk of clashing with the United States at a time when the very survival of the state was under grave danger. Israel could by no means assume that her military victory was assured, since the leading assumption at this stage was that the outcome of such a military confrontation was unknown.[10]

Israel had to assume that it would probably "end up" needing political, military and economic support from the United States. Another possibility, probably less dangerous for Israel in the immediate future, would be to comply with Washington's "dictate" to refrain from carrying out a military response against Egypt, meaning that practically Israel accepted the unilateral changes in the status quo forced by President Nasser. In effect, this would result in a major political-strategic defeat for Israel.[11]

Beyond the uncertainties concerning the benefit of a political mission of this kind, Eshkol, and apparently other ministers as well, had grave doubts whether Abba Eban was suited to the job. Officially the mission was unquestionably suited for him; he was serving in two capacities, Deputy Prime Minister and Foreign Minister. Over the years Eban had been Israel's ambassador to the United States and the United Nations, and was therefore very familiar with the political arena in the US. His verbal skill in English was his international "calling card", and his close ties to the American Jewish community in the United States would undoubtedly assist him greatly during this critical period. Assuming that the Prime Minister did not wish to go on the mission (this option was not even raised for discussion), the next in line was naturally the Deputy Prime Minister and Foreign Minister.[12]

These considerations were valid in normal times, and even in normal crises, but the current events were exceptionally grave from every perspective. Since the end of the War of 1948, no Arab country had dared to challenge Israel so blatantly. Egypt must have been fully aware that its initiatives were brazenly aggressive, since the crisis had created the sense of an existential threat in the Israeli leadership and the entire country. Whether this feeling was objectively justified was irrelevant at this point. As noted, Abba Eban was a statesman highly skilled in dramatic public appearances, with outstanding rhetorical skills. He was also known, however, for his restrained approach and his fastidiousness in the rules of diplomatic etiquette. Eshkol felt that under the present circumstances a different type of personality was required, someone capable of departing from "rules of protocol", capable of banging on tables and shaking up the international system in general, particularly the Johnson administration.[13]

According to available accounts, Eshkol wanted to send Golda Meir on this mission, even though her title was only Secretary-General of Mapai. Her political–diplomatic experience was impeccable; she had served as Israel's ambassador to the Soviet Union after the War of 1948, and as Foreign Minister prior to and following the Sinai Campaign. Furthermore, her main assets under the prevailing circumstances were her assertive Jewish background and electrifying personality. Perhaps more than any other figure in the Israeli political elite, Golda Meir was capable of placing this crisis in the historical context of the Jewish people's millennia-long struggle for survival. Her authority and demeanor could mobilize the American Jewish community to apply unbearable pressure on the American administration.[14]

In the final analysis, Ms. Meir's presence in the United States would have confronted the administration with a most unenviable dilemma if it chose to retract its commitments to Israel. There could be no doubt that she was the better choice under the prevailing circumstances. Eban, however, was probably the last personage who would forgo this historical opportunity to save the country at this crucial moment. Over the years he had radiated vaunting self-esteem in his statements and diplomatic activity; therefore it was natural that he would fight "tooth and nail" against removing the mission from his authority, even threatening resignation if someone else was assigned the task. Prime Minister Eshkol, who had no interest in triggering an internal crisis – in addition to the external one – was forced to accept Eban's demand.[15]

On the eve of Eban's departure on his diplomatic mission (May 23), President Johnson delivered a speech to the nation in which he expressed his government's efforts to restrain Israel and temper its responses. At the same time, he also mentioned the administration's growing awareness that Nasser's steps not only threatened Israel, but also the vital interests and international position of the United States. The president pointed out that there were three combustible factors in the crisis: (a) Militant activity taking place from the territory of one country against another (infiltration and acts of violence against Israel); (b) The hasty evacuation of UN forces from Sinai and the Gaza Strip; and (c) The massive build-up of forces on both sides.[16]

Furthermore, the president stated, "a new and very grave dimension" had recently been added to the equation: the blockade of the Straits of Tiran to Israeli shipping. The president made clear that the United States viewed the Straits of Tiran as an international waterway, therefore their blockade to Israeli vessels was "illegal and potentially dangerous to the cause of peace". The right to freedom of navigation in the Straits was of vital interest to the international system, the president stressed. The US was committed to the peace and territorial integrity of the states in the region and rejected an aggressive act by any side, whether made openly or covertly. The United States asked all of the countries in the area to exhibit restraint.[17]

The following day, May 24, the National Security Council convened for a special meeting on the Middle East crisis. From the protocol we learn that the administration lacked a well-formulated situation estimate on Nasser's aims. Initially he seemed to have sought a grandiose political achievement that would boost his international and regional status without entailing a military confrontation. However, the closure of the Straits completely changed the picture since it contained the palpable risk of entanglement in a military clash with Israel. The participants in the meeting realized that Nasser knew that he could not retreat without seriously damaging his political stature. His latest moves attested to the fact that he was not employing his usual modus operandi, that left him an "escape hatch" if something went amiss. This time it was difficult to explain the nature of his motives.[18]

Administration officials had two possible explanations for Nasser's moves: (a) The Soviet Union had guaranteed Nasser backing that no one in the West had knowledge of; and (b) President Nasser was acting irresponsibly or irrationally. An analysis of the administration's statements at this stage reveals that it tended to believe that, under those severe circumstances, Israel's only choice was to respond militarily to Egypt's steps. It appeared that Washington failed to acknowledge the likelihood that some political circles in Israel would prefer to avoid an armed clash by reaching some kind of arrangement that would satisfy Egypt. Such an arrangement might include, for example, placing Israel's nuclear facilities under international observation in exchange for Egyptian readiness to allow free Israeli shipping through the Straits of Tiran. The Egyptian leadership may also have been prepared for such a scenario, and did not see war as the only escape from the crisis.[19]

At the start of the meeting, Secretary of State, Dean Rusk, announced that the situation was "serious but not yet desperate". He then discussed the reports from the Deputy Secretary-General of the UN, Ralph Bunche, regarding Egypt's conditions for exiting the crisis via a return to the Armistice Agreements that had been in effect prior to the Sinai Campaign. In Rusk's opinion, Israel would reject these conditions. The Secretary of State told of secret meetings with the Soviet leadership in which the Kremlin had expressed a moderate and pragmatic position. Still, the official Soviet hard line placed responsibility for the crisis directly on Israel, and indirectly on the United States. Rusk also noted that the Egyptians and Syrians claimed that the Soviet Union was fully supporting them, but estimated that it was not acting unconditionally.[20]

The administration's treasury minister, Henry Fowler, suggested considering economic steps in conjunction with the World Bank and other international organizations as a solution to the crisis. In practical terms, this meant threatening Egypt with economic sanctions for its closure of the Straits of Tiran. Fowler believed that an Israeli military operation could be averted if it was convinced that an armed strike against Egypt would cause greater harm than the damage from the maritime blockade. The Secretary of State had reservations over this proposal; his general approach was that the administration must not act unilaterally in the crisis, but should act in coordination with the UN and other states.[21]

Johnson agreed with this position in principle but stated emphatically that he did not expect UN assistance in solving the crisis. Although he intended to cooperate with Britain and France, he felt the administration's chances for unilateral action should be examined in the eventuality that the options for working within a wider framework failed. Finally, the president had qualms over the view expressed by a number of senators that the US was unable to deal with two crises simultaneously, and that it had to decide if it wanted to focus on Southeast Asia (Vietnam) or the Middle East. Johnson wanted congressional leaders to know that such statements played into the hands of the Soviets in this vexing crisis.[22]

In the course of the debate, General Earle Wheeler, the chairman of the Joint Chiefs of Staff, stated that he was incredibly reluctant to see the United States directly involved in the Middle East crisis. He believed that opening the Straits would be far more difficult than it first appeared, since two Egyptian submarines were based in the Red Sea. This would require the US Navy to deploy anti-submarine vessels in the region. Such equipment was located in Singapore, and could reach the area only in two weeks. While the United States had a strong naval force in the region, its ground force was very limited (1,400 marines stationed in Nepal) and could arrive in the region in three days. Wheeler further pointed out that the United States would have problems getting more forces to the region because of the opposition of certain countries – such as Spain, Turkey, and Libya – that would refuse to help it move against Egypt. According to Wheeler, Israel had no need of foreign forces to attain its goals, it could "solve" the crisis on its own.[23]

Wheeler estimated that if Israel decided on a military operation to open the Straits, it would commence with an air strike against the Egyptian fleet in the Red Sea and Egyptian airbases in Sinai. Only after it attained air superiority would it try to gain control of the Sharm el-Sheikh area and open the Straits; therefore from Israel's perspective a limited military operation in the Straits of Tiran area was impractical. As for the employment of non-conventional weapons in the region, the general reminded his listeners that the Egyptians had used gas in Yemen. Richard Helms, the director of the CIA, claimed that no state in the Middle East had nuclear capability, a statement whose accuracy was questioned by Wheeler. By Wheeler's account, the United States should be satisfied in extending assistance to Israel without committing itself to direct involvement in the crisis.[24]

The discussion reveals that the various branches of American administration had solid information on Israel's military plans. Washington apparently knew that Israel would launch an air offensive, designed to smash the Egyptian air force and achieve air superiority in the initial stages of the confrontation. It is interesting to note that several days later, in a joint American situation estimate, Defense Secretary McNamara stated that an Israeli operation would commence with an air strike intended to neutralize the Egyptian air force. As stated, our impression is that these views reflected not only military estimates of Israel's offensive plans, but also reliable information obtained by the US.[25]

During the meeting Johnson wanted to know, in the case of a showdown in the Mideast, how accurate the estimate was regarding Israel's military superiority vis-à-vis the Arabs. He reminded those present that Arthur Goldberg's (the American ambassador to the UN) assessment had raised doubts regarding Israeli military superiority. The president insisted on learning what the United States could do if all attempts at resolving the crisis peacefully failed. Richard Helms and General Wheeler promised to reexamine their estimates on the matter. General Wheeler stated that Israeli military action might create a protracted confrontation with the Arab states, therefore the administration had to converse with Israel concerning its military and economic needs in the case of a prolonged struggle as soon as possible. Israel currently had enough fighting material for thirty days, the general declared, but later the White House might have to consider the possibility of direct military involvement.[26]

In answer to the president's question, Wheeler replied that American military involvement in the conflict would not necessarily precipitate Soviet intervention. Richard Helms accepted the main lines of Wheeler's assessment, since both Helms and Wheeler believed that the Soviet Union had not planned the crisis, instead viewing it as something that served its interests. McNamara disagreed with this estimate, stating that if hostilities erupted the air forces of both sides would be seriously incapacitated and would require rearmament. In this case, each side would undoubtedly turn to the superpowers for succor. As the Defense Secretary saw it, the Kremlin would transfer Soviet-manned fighter squadrons to Egypt.[27]

The CIA director disagreed with this estimate, asserting that Israel's air superiority was guaranteed. He recalled that Israel had "netted" a Mig-21 and was very familiar with it. The reference, of course, was to the 1966 windfall of getting an Iraqi pilot to fly an Iraqi air force Mig-21 to Israel. McNamara also mentioned the April 7, 1967, air skirmish in which six Syrian Mig-21s were shot down to one Israeli plane damaged.[28]

As the meeting drew to a close, the president suddenly asked whether Foreign Minister Eban had arrived in Washington to meet with him, an immensely baffling question. The administration must have known that the objective of Eban's trip was a meeting with the president, as this was the only way Eban could learn of the United States' exact position and intentions in the crisis. Less surprising is the president's ancillary question, that is, should he agree to Eban's request for a meeting. [29]

As we shall shortly see, Johnson did not "appreciate" Eban's mission to Washington as an event that would serve US interests at this time. He was undoubtedly aware that such a meeting put the United States' status in the Middle East, and its relations with the Arab world, at risk. Furthermore, a meeting at such a high level was liable to compel the administration to define its positions and "ground" plans in more operational terms. The administration had no interest in doing this, especially not at the present stage.[30]

Under-Secretary of State, Eugene Rostow, said with assurance, as could be expected, that Eban would definitely request such a meeting, since it was the *raison d'être* of his entire mission. Rostow tried to avoid determining whether the meeting was desirable for the United States. However, he did admit that the Israeli government had initiated its foreign minister's trip to the United States in order to forestall an impending military response to Egypt's closure of the Straits. For this reason he advised the president to meet with Eban. Rostow's reply indicated, indirectly albeit, that Johnson's question had been beside the point. The president had no choice but to meet with Eban, and this is indeed what happened.[31]

At 3:30 in the morning of May 24, Eban embarked upon his fateful trip to the West. Accompanied by his personal secretary, Moshe Raviv, in an El Al aircraft, Eban arrived in Paris in the early hours of the morning for talks with President De Gaulle. In meetings between American and French officials, the French informed their counterparts that they regarded the blockage of the Straits of Tiran as an extremely serious incident. In a discussion between the American ambassador to France, Charles Bohlen, and the director of the French foreign ministry, Herve Alphand, the latter pointed out that Israel would attack Egypt in all likelihood.[32]

Statements by Israel and other parties in the West, following Israel's pullback from Sinai in 1957, had created a situation that made it difficult to accept the new reality in Sinai and the Red Sea. Alphand explained that France did not think that the terms of the Tripartite Declaration, drawn up by the three Western superpowers in the early 1950s, had to be reaffirmed. Reemphasizing the authority of the declaration at the present hour might only embitter and alienate the Arab world. France favored formal consultation among all of the superpowers, including the Soviet Union, without being fettered to a particular declaration.[33]

In hindsight, it is difficult to fathom Eban's determination to meet De Gaulle; France's position on the crisis, and especially De Gaulle's, were well known since they had been conveyed in public addresses and closed-door talks. Israel was far from satisfied with France's positions, since France vigorously opposed a military operation for restoring the *status quo ante*, believing that "crisis management" should be left to the superpowers. No one had any illusions that Israel would consent to an arrangement that was acceptable to the Soviet Union. [34]

It is doubtful that Eban believed he could sway De Gaulle to Israel's side (the French president was noted for his intractable stubbornness regarding a solution to the crisis). Even before Eban's meeting with De Gaulle, the French Foreign Minister, Couve de Murville, informed Israel's ambassador to France, Walter Eitan, of the trends that were crystallizing in France's position. "The first thing," de Murville told Ambassador Eitan, "is to understand the Russians' intentions and bring them to fruition . . . The main task is to include the Soviet Union [in consultations] since the key [to solving the crisis] lies in its hands."[35]

De Murville stressed France's conviction that the solution to the crisis had to be approached in a practical manner, rather than leaving it bound to legal and political principles. Israel's problem, as de Murville perceived it, was not the blockade of the Straits of Tiran and the abrogation of the basic right of navigation through the Straits, but the losses that would be incurred as a result of Egypt's aggressive move. The main problem facing Israel after the closure of the Straits was the importation of oil. In any case, there were no Israeli warships based in Eilat, therefore a practical solution to the problem had to be found.[36]

In this pinched and unfavorable atmosphere Eban entered the meeting with President De Gaulle. "To the credit" of the French it must be said that they did not hide their views of the crisis and the means of solving it, therefore the need for the meeting appears even more incomprehensible. According to Eban's account, immediately on entering De Gaulle's office, and even before he had time to sit down and present his opening statement, De Gaulle preempted him, declaring, "Do not fight. Let the four superpowers resolve the conflict. France will influence the Soviet Union to adopt an amenable position toward peace." De Gaulle's brusque and definitive manner, which deviated from the rules of protocol that he customarily abided by, was undoubtedly intended to emphasize France's determination to oppose an Israeli-initiated military act. Later the president repeated his position. During the meeting Eban tried to temper De Gaulle's positions toward Israel by showering him with gratitude for France's assistance in the crisis. Our impression is that, despite his Sisyphean efforts, Eban failed to generate a more affable atmosphere in the meeting.[37]

Other reports on the Eban–De Gaulle talk that were sent to Israel, as far as can be determined, were sketchy and fragmentary. During the course of the conversation the French president stressed the following points: (a) Israel must not commence hostilities (but it could retaliate if attacked). Another report quoted de Gaulle as saying, "It would be a catastrophe if Israel initiated military operations"; (b) Israel must leave the solution of the main issues to the four superpowers. According to another report De Gaulle stated, that "an effort must be made to open the Straits by an international body whose first step will be quadrilateral consultations"; (c) France will proceed with all means available to influence the Soviet Union to adopt positions that will lead to a peaceful solution to the crisis; (d) The more that Israel relies solely on the West, the less the Soviet Union will be inclined to cooperate, and the less likelihood there will be for a solution to the crisis; and (e) Nasser and the Soviet Union are interested in having Israel initiate hostilities, therefore Israel must not provide them with the satisfaction.[38]

Two days before the war broke out President de Gaulle met with the Israeli ambassador to France. Eitan's report of the conversation seemed to express De Gaulle's "true" position on the crisis. The president's wording was blunt and unequivocal regarding all aspects of Israel's expected response. According to Eitan, De Gaulle made the following remarks, alternately employing the first person and third person pronoun. "It has always been obvious that the Arabs wish to destroy us [the State of Israel]. But due to our strength they have been unable to [accomplish this]. This time too they will not destroy us. He [De Gaulle] believes that war will bring a catastrophe upon us even if we win. We will suffer heavy losses. The Arabs will bomb our cities, and in the end instead of solving the problem we will only magnify hatred. Also, the Arabs must not be allowed to go to war against Israel since it will be a catastrophe for them and us."[39]

"At present," De Gaulle further stressed, "everyone is over-excited. If the crisis passes without war the basic problems may be solved, mainly, the Gulf problem [the Straits of Tiran]. Perhaps, after this grave crisis, Israel will be recognized by those who currently do not recognize it, including the Arabs, and we may attain [peaceful] relations with our neighbors. Nasser will need material assistance and will be happy to receive it even from the United States. Do not rely too much on the United States, it may work to our benefit [in the short run] but it will soon come up against the oil problem and [closure of the canal], and then [its enthusiasm to help Israel] will cool . . . [Today] is not 1957 [the Sinai Campaign and the French–Israeli pact]. Then he [De Gaulle] was not in power, and the times have changed too. France has renewed its relations with the Arab world and is interested in improving them."[40]

During the talk, De Gaulle repeated his warning against an Israeli-initiated strike, reiterating that the only way to solve the crisis was through a superpower agreement. In the first stages of the crisis the Soviet Union had expressed its reservation over superpower cooperation; now it was displaying its willingness to take part in the effort to find a solution. France wanted Israel to survive as a state, not to disappear. As for its decision to place an embargo on weapons to Israel, De Gaulle made it clear that the embargo would remain in effect as long as it was uncertain if Israel would embark upon war. "After the crisis, France would renew its supply as before. Its refusal to provide us with weapons was designed to influence us not to go to war." De Gaulle deliberately ignored the ambassador's two arguments:

1. While France refused Israel weapons, the Soviet Union continued to supply arms to the Arabs;
2. France's refusal to sell weapons to Israel may have been intended to prevent it from initiating an attack, however the possibility remained that it might hasten Israel's decision to go to war.[41]

After the Eban meeting, De Gaulle decided to halt arms supplies to Israel. The question will always remain open: Did their meeting contribute to De Gaulle's decision to undertake such a severe measure at a very critical time for Israel? Did Eban's congratulatory remarks to De Gaulle for French military assistance to Israel turn on a "red light", bringing him to realize that France's arms supplies to Israel might be seen as the main cause for Israel's "intransigent" positions in the crisis? Or would the De Gaulle government have made this decision all the same, regardless of what Eban said? De Gaulle made clear to Eitan that "the ban [on weapons supplies] would remain in force as long as it was unclear if we are embarking on war. Afterwards the supply would be renewed." Eitan informed President De Gaulle that this decision gravely hurt Israel because the Soviet Union continued to supply weapons to the Arab states.[42]

Immediately after the frustrating meeting with De Gaulle, Eban flew to Britain for a considerably more relaxed meeting with Prime Minister Harold Wilson. Britain expressed sympathetic understanding of Israel's situation and took a stauncher position on the freedom of navigation through the Straits than the other super-powers, including the United States. In the course of the meeting Eban explained to Wilson that Israel faced three choices: surrender to Nasser, war with Nasser, or give the superpowers a chance to solve the crisis by political means, with a solution that included freedom of shipping through the Straits. Eban made it clear to his listener that surrendering to Nasser was not an option. Nevertheless, the Israeli Foreign Minister emphasized the economic factor involved in the closing of the Straits, avowing that Israel could not survive without the Port of Eilat since it was an essential part of the country's economic lifeblood.[43]

It is unclear why Eban stressed the economic aspect of the conflict and presented it as the main reason for Israel's insistence on navigational freedom in the Straits of Tiran. Eban must have known the unlikelihood of this claim being considered sufficient justifica-tion for a belligerent move by Israel. The Western countries could charge that economic damages required economic compensation, but that they certainly did not warrant the initiation of hostilities. In addition, they could rightly claim that Israel had subsisted for many years without port facilities in Eilat and had progressed remarkably well. Therefore, in our opinion, Eban's presentation of the cessa-tion of such facilities as a "question of survival" would not be received with much credibility. Actually, Nasser's steps were crit-ical because they expressed the bankruptcy of Israel's deterrent capability; he made this move fully aware that Israel and the Western superpowers would see it as a pretext for war. The lack of suitable response by Israel could only be interpreted as a grave blow to her strategic credibility.[44]

Eban warned the British prime minister that if Israel was left with no other choice, it would fight even if it had to "go at it" alone. Eban believed that Israel would emerge victorious, but the results would be tragic for both sides. Israel did not desire war, he emphasized, instead it sought a political solution to the crisis. He recalled the superpower's commitment after Israel's withdrawal from Sinai in 1957 to guarantee freedom of navigation in the Straits of Tiran. Eban bitterly criticized U Thant, the UN Secretary-General, for acquiescing to Nasser's demand to evacuate the UN forces from Sinai, stressing that in ten minutes U Thant had destroyed a ten-year enterprise. Eban described the current mood in Israel as "calm resolution". Being fully aware of the grave fears in Israel, as Eban certainly was, it is doubtful whether he believed what he was saying.[45]

According to Eban, from both an operational and psychological perspective, Egypt must not be the only party with naval forces in the Red Sea. He admitted that in its present state the Israeli navy was temporarily not as strong as the Egyptian navy, implying that Israel was not capable of coping with the Egyptian naval force by itself. His message was clear: the superpowers would have to supply the requisite naval forces in the Red Sea. The closure of the Straits, he stated, posed a major threat not only to Israel but also to the Hashemite regime in Jordan, since Nasser could block ships to the port in Akaba whenever he desired.[46]

Eban knew that Britain had a vital interest in the preservation of this pro-Western regime, praising its willingness to assist Israel by immediately sending arms. According to Eban's account, Wilson informed him that the British government had convened that morning to discuss the crisis, and had come to a general agreement that Nasser's blockade policy must not be allowed to triumph. Britain would cooperate with other states in a joint effort to open the Straits.[47]

9

Abba Eban's Mission: Phase II
Talks with Key Officials

Immediately after his most satisfying meeting with Prime Minister Wilson, Eban set out on his main mission – a talk with President Johnson in Washington. Arriving in the United States at one o'clock in the afternoon of May 25, 1967, Eban learned that the deck had been reshuffled and that the basic assumptions which had prevailed on the eve of his journey were no longer valid. Eban received a frantic message from Eshkol stating that, according to Israel's latest intelligence assessment, an all-out UAR–Syrian attack was imminent. Four Egyptian infantry divisions were now in Sinai, as were two armored divisions comprising eight hundred tanks.[1]

Eban realized that under these circumstances the freedom of navigation issue – the "original" reason for his mission – had now become secondary, with Israel facing a far greater and more palpable threat: a combined Egyptian–Syrian onslaught. Against this background, Eban was instructed to try to skip talks at the administration's professional level and make an utmost effort to receive an immediate audience with President Johnson. If that was impossible, then he should at least try to meet the Secretary of State. Eshkol asked Eban to present the American government with two concrete demands:

1 An American announcement at the highest level that an attack against Israel would be considered an attack against the United States.
2 An order from the administration to its forces in the region to coordinate their activity with the IDF so as to forestall such an attack.[2]

Currently available information suggests that Abba Eban doubted the accuracy of the information in the message. He may have regarded it as an attempt by certain elements in the Israeli secu-rity establishment to precipitate a military confrontation at as early a date as possible, by forcing the government to make an immediate decision in this direction. Eban was known as one of the principle advocates of the political track, even if it meant taking moderate military risks.[3]

Knowledge of an impending two-pronged Egyptian–Syrian attack would force the political leadership to decide immediately on preventive military action. The only way to avoid such a decision would be by acquiring a determined commitment on the part of the administration to defend Israel in the event of a military showdown. The White House's disinclination, as could be expected, to provide Israel with the security backing it desperately sought would most probably lead the Israeli government to opt for a swift military oper-ation, which the military establishment vigorously demanded. It was obvious that a nerve-wracking, passive wait for an Egyptian attack contained risks that no one in the Israeli leadership wished to bear responsibility for.[4]

In his book, *Chapters in my Life*, Eban describes the difficult dilemmas he faced because of the Prime Minister's message, swinging like a pendulum between two options. On the one hand, he seriously doubted the truth of the military assessment. He also suspected that the message was intended to serve the strategic objec-tives of militant circles in Israel to compel the government to decide to launch a preventive war against Egypt. If so, then he would have to ignore the message or relegate it to the sidelines. On the other hand, he could by no means rule out the possibility that the estimate was accurate. In such a case, ignoring Eshkol's message or dimin-ishing its importance might lead to a catastrophic disaster for Israel.[5]

In another book written many years later, Eban sounded much more certain about the low credibility of message, stating that the message conveyed false information. Against this background, and in light of the message's grave ramifications for American–Israeli relations, Eban did not hesitate to challenge the Prime Minister's missive. He criticized it bitterly, referring to the challenge as an expression of "momentous irresponsibility". Eban broadly hinted that the message was based on inaccuracies and that the heads of the military had "manipulated" Eshkol to sign it. He recalled that on the eve of his departure, the assessments of the Israeli intelligence community stressed that the Egyptian forces were widely spread across Sinai and plagued by severe logistical problems. How could one presume, Eban queried, that within a few hours so drastic a volte-face could occur in the situation estimate?[6]

On May 24, 1967, a few hours after Eban embarked on his mission, Ambassador Barbour was called to the Prime Minister's office to meet with Shlomo Argov and Aryeh Levavi, foreign ministry officials. The two immediately made it clear that they had come to the meeting at a "moment of grave peril [for the State of Israel]". They informed the American ambassador that Eban had received a frantic memo, ordering him to explain to the highest levels of government in Washington that an Egyptian attack against Israel was "imminent", and that the United States should demonstrate its commitment to Israel by official declarations and military activity.[7]

Barbour suspected at once that he was being told this information because the Israelis were preparing a possible attack against Egypt and other Arab states. The information conveyed to him was meant to serve as a justification for Israel's attack. If the US would not accept these demands, it would have a moral obligation to let Israel defend itself, at least. Barbour expressed surprise at the dramatic transformation in the Israeli position on such short notice, especially when on the previous day it had decided to test the political track for solving the crisis.[8]

Argov and Bitan apparently failed to convince Barbour that the turnabout in Israel's assessment had occurred because of a radical change in Egypt's intentions and deployment in Sinai. Our impression is that Barbour intuited that Israel's "hawks" breathed a sigh of relief once Eban left the country. They seemed to have assessed that with his departure, one of the main obstacles to getting governmental approval for military action had been removed, and the time was ripe "to move" before circumstances changed. In this situation, Ambassador Barbour pointed out that an Israeli-initiated strike, while its foreign minister was on route to Washington to explore the options of a diplomatic solution to the crisis, would have "disastrous" repercussions. It seems Barbour implied that such a move would be a gross affront to the American administration in general and the president of the United States in particular.[9]

Once in Washington, Eban realized that all the American intelligence agencies were of the same opinion regarding Egypt's military deployment in Sinai. Their assessment stressed that Egypt's deployment was basically defensive and there was no sign of a planned offensive against Israel. This estimate corresponded with Egypt's position, which had been clarified to Washington, that Egypt had no intention of initiating a military step, despite its awareness that Israel might be planning such a move. The reiteration of this view seemed to have been an indirect signal to Israel that it had no reason to panic over an Egyptian preemptive strike; instead it could proceed with relative calm to obtain the best results if it opted for a military strike.[10]

Eban met with Secretary of Defense Robert McNamara and General Earle Wheeler, chairman of the Joint Chiefs of Staff, laying out the three main factors behind the crisis: (a) Terrorist attacks emanating from Syria against Israel; (b) The concentration of Egyptian forces in Sinai and the evacuation of UN forces from the peninsula; and (c) The blockade of the Straits of Tiran. The removal of the UN forces, he predicted, would prove to be a historical error, but the immediate danger to Israel was the closure of the Straits.[11]

This act, the foreign minister claimed, had changed the geopolitical parameter of the Arab–Israeli conflict, making it much more serious than terrorist attacks and the concentration of Egyptian forces. The blockage to the Port of Eilat paralyzed Israel and cut it off from half the world. Furthermore, Israel's claims against the blockade of the Straits were based on a weighty legal argument and the fact that thousands of vessels had travelled through the Straits over the last decade. By way of example, this was comparable to blockading all of the United States' ports and commercial lanes along the Atlantic Ocean.[12]

Nasser, Eban continued, tried to deny Israel this right with a flick of the wrist, stressing that the closure of the Straits was a *casus belli*. Eban told the Americans that, before his departure for the mission, the Israeli government had met and decided to oppose the blockage of the Straits and not to cede this issue. Israel would not accept a situation that would compel her to go on living with only one lung. The exact meaning of this metaphor escapes us; Eban may have meant that the Port of Eilat was one of Israel's two maritime links to the outside world, the second lung being the Port of Haifa. If the Straits of Tiran were closed to Israeli shipping it would be the end of the Port of Eilat.[13]

Eban continued to say that Israel had decided to postpone a military operation in order to study the proposal of establishing an international maritime force for reopening the Straits. Naturally, this was a one dimensional, partially accurate interpretation of the

May 23 government meeting. The mood in the meeting, even at the military level, was restrained regarding a military strike. Eban, who actually led the moderate course, was probably more aware of this than others. However, at this moment he wanted to depict Israel as though it was dead set on launching a military campaign to retrieve its navigational rights. Its agreement to cancel military parades depended, of course, on Washington's willingness to accept responsibility for guaranteeing maritime freedom through the Straits.[14]

Eban said that his mission was to examine the practicality of this proposal and the steps that Britain and the United States intended to take to realize it. Israel was convinced, he stated, that the US could implement the reopening of the Straits with minimal risk, however it is unclear what Eban based so definitive an assertion on. He proposed that a number of vessels of the American Sixth Fleet escort Israeli ships moving through the Straits of Tiran.[15]

He ignored, understandably, the complications liable to beset such an operation, failing to mention the escort's timeframe, for example. Would the United States be willing to accompany Israeli vessels for a lengthy period of time? What exactly was the US supposed to do if the Egyptians opened fire on ships carrying the Israeli flag or blocked their passage to Eilat? Was the United States willing to get involved in a confrontation with Egypt at a time when it was mired up to its neck in the Vietnam War?[16]

Eban recalled the American commitment to protect Israeli navigation in the Straits. During the conversation he was handed a section of a document from February 26, 1957, and began to read it aloud. The section included, *inter alia*, a declaration by the former Secretary of State, John Foster Dulles, stating that the United States would defend freedom of navigation through the Straits of Tiran. Eban's reading of the document seems to have caused the Americans considerable discomfort, since the transfer of the document to Eban during the talks added an unjustified flavor of dramatics to the proceedings. Whatever the case, it was clear that the last thing the administration wanted now was public quibbling over legalities with Israel on the nature of the implementation of a guarantee that it had signed.[17]

The White House officials did not reject Israel's claim that the United States had pledged to protect freedom of navigation through the Straits. This course of action was undertaken despite legal arguments involved that could allow Washington, if it really wished, to "wiggle out" of the implementation of its commitment. Under the circumstances prevailing at this period of time, public opinion in the West, including the United States, tended to enthusiastically support Israel's positions on the freedom of navigation issue, whatever the exact wording of US pledges were.[18]

Therefore, any attempt to ignore the United States' guarantee would encounter widespread condemnation. The best course the administration could undertake in such circumstances was to ask Israel to avoid exploiting this issue, since it placed the administration in a most embarrassing position. Eban was keenly aware of the White House's request, but chose to ignore it, having no alternative if he wished to prevent the outbreak of a war. He knew that an American refusal to stand by its commitments would compel Israel to undertake military course, but it is doubtful whether this tactic helped him on such a sensitive diplomatic mission.[19]

Under these circumstances, McNamara justifiably chose to ignore Eban's assertions, refraining from discussion on the American commitment to the freedom of navigation through the Straits. In effect, he had no practical alternative to offer, unable to deny the truth of the statements. On the other hand, if he affirmed them, he would have to explain how the United States intended to actualize them. Therefore he chose a more convenient issue from his point of view – the practical aspects involved in realizing the American obligation, effectively responding to Eban with "an eye for an eye". Just as Eban had chosen, to no avail, to reiterate Washington's commitment to freedom of navigation through the Straits, the US too could regurgitate issues that Israel regarded as a waste of time.[20]

McNamara's question to Eban in this context was: how long would vessels from the American fleet have to escort Israeli-flagged ships through the Straits of Tiran? The American Defense Secretary considered himself justified in emphasizing the major drawback in Israel's request that Washington realize its obligation. He did not have to elaborate his argument; even if the United States succeeded in getting Israeli vessels through the Straits, the success would be of limited duration. Obviously, Israel could not expect the US to leave its naval force in the Straits "forever", therefore the question McNamara was actually asking Eban was: how exactly would the presence of the American fleet in the Red Sea help in the long run?[21]

Eban was at a loss to come up with an answer, merely mumbling about the importance in immediately realizing the commitment so that a new status quo would not set in. As time passed it would become increasingly difficult to change the existing status quo. A similar situation developed in the case of freedom of navigation in the Suez Canal. According to Eban, Egypt would eventually be interested in removing the American naval presence from the region so as not to appear as the side that had yielded to the might of a superpower. Under these circumstances, Eban predicted (and it is not clear upon what evidence) that Egypt would soon permit Israel freedom of navigation even without a tight American escort.[22]

McNamara was much less optimistic. He believed that the permanent Egyptian presence in the Straits did not involve great costs, therefore it could remain in the area for a long period. At this point, Eban seemed to have begun losing his patience, understanding that the administration wanted to tire him out in talks that were futile from Israel's perspective regarding the practical aspects of a plan that no one had even drafted.[23]

Under these circumstances, Eban had no choice but to attempt to revert the discussion back to lines convenient for him, noting that "immediate action" needed to be taken by the United States without any "worries" about its consequences. This move, he stressed, had to be independent of the participation of any other states. Eban apparently felt that he was not making a strong impression on his listeners with such a course of argumentation, therefore he decided to play what he believed was his "trump card". He threatened that unless American commitments for "ultimate action" were honored, Israel would act unilaterally and "the balloon would go up next week".[24]

Eban's threats that Israel would carry out a preemptive strike point to his severe break from the administration's position following the closure of the Straits. He seemed to have been acting according to an assumption that had been valid in the early stages of the crisis, at a time when Washington had tried its utmost to restrain Israel from launching a military operation against Egypt. Now, following the blockage of the Straits, a dramatic turnabout had taken place in the White House's position. Influential members of the Johnson Administration now believed Nasser's moves were directed not only against Israel, but also against the United States. There could be no doubt that if the blockade would become fait accompli, US prestige and credibility would suffer an extremely severe blow.

Consequently, the administration gradually reached the conclusion that there was no turning back from a military confrontation, and that it was best to let Israel move against Egypt. The White House's main interest at this stage was to prevent "insinuations" linking the United States to Israeli military steps. It wanted Israel to infer where America's interests lay without recourse to mentioning them explicitly.

In this light, Eban's saber-rattling showed his misreading or ignorance of the signals being emitted from the administration's corridors. Another possibility is that Eban purposely chose to "misinterpret" the signal. He realized that the Johnson Administration wanted "to push" Israel into a military adventure that could serve American interests while the United States sat "on the sidelines", plucking the fruit whose price and risks were being paid for by Israel. Eban probably wanted to avoid the war that was looming on the horizon, explaining why he preferred to act as though he failed to "pick up" the White House's messages, whether overt or implied, that Israel was "allowed" to "go at it alone".

McNamara, as one could expect, made no reply to Eban's strong words and explicit threats of Israeli military activity in the near future. Having no alternative, Eban switched to a different line of argument that also turned out to be ineffectual too. He claimed that Washington's position on its commitment to guarantee freedom of navigation in the Straits was the acid test for American credibility in the entire international arena. Eban added in a provocative tone that on the agenda stood the question of America's ability to realize its commitments in the Middle East at a time when it was deeply involved in the War in Vietnam. He should have known that these words touched upon a very sensitive topic in the administration's nerve system. Indeed, McNamara appeared to have been somewhat offended by this reproach, telling Eban that no one need doubt the United States' determination to honor its commitments and its military strength.[25]

McNamara went on to say that the United States first had to exhaust the political course. Practically this meant going through the auspices of the UN and gaining the support of Congress and public opinion before deciding on a military solution. Concerned that these statements might be interpreted by Eban as Washington's consent to an Israeli attack, the American Defense Secretary hastened to clarify that under the present circumstances the United States opposed an Israeli-initiated preemptive strike. He did not, however, explain the term "present circumstances". He seemed to have been referring to an Israeli operation prior to the exhaustion of all the political channels to solving the crisis. McNamara warned that if Israel decided, nonetheless, to make the first move, there were liable to be incredibly serious repercussions (again his words remained vague).[26]

At this stage in the conversation Ambassador Harman was called to the telephone. When he returned he announced that he had been informed, most likely by the Prime Minister and Defense Minister, that Israeli intelligence had received information of an "imminent" Egyptian–Syrian attack on Israel. This dramatic announcement appeared to jolt Eban into remembering that he was supposed to highlight this issue, rather than freedom of navigation in the Straits of Tiran. Eban grabbed at this opportunity, making it clear that this was not a situation estimate, but a case of solid information. Later he was more precise, stating that this was not just regular data but factual "knowledge" of an immediate attack.[27]

McNamara informed Eban that the information in the administration's hands was different, and more importantly, incompatible with the Israeli information. According to American intelligence branches, the Egyptian forces in Sinai were deployed defensively against an Israeli first strike. At this point in the conversation General Wheeler intervened, asking whether the term "knowledge" that Eban used expressed definite knowledge. Eban equivocated, only reaffirming that it was a case of knowledge – and not intelligence-based information. According to his distinction between "knowledge" and "information", it turns out that this was a case of definite knowledge.[28]

Available sources show that McNamara's statements on the credibility of the Israeli information regarding an imminent Egyptian–Syrian attack were phrased with extreme circumspection. The estimate of the administration's intelligence agencies, it should be stressed, was much blunter. A top-secret memo of the State Department's Research and Intelligence Branch specifically stated that the claim of an impending Arab attack against Israel was "an incorrect reading of the situation estimate, if not an intentional falsification and distortion of reality". [29]

According to the administration, the information that Israel conveyed, especially the urgency of its tone, indicated Israel's intention to launch a preventive strike against Egypt. The statements being relayed to the White House on all aspects of an approaching

Egyptian–Syrian attack were designed to prepare the way for the justification of Israel's preventive strike. This was a singularly sharp accusation against the messages being sent from the highest political-security level in Israel.[30]

An estimation of the Israeli message, in light of our actual knowledge of the Egyptian deployment prior to the outbreak of the war, leaves no doubt that it was a misreading of the facts, perhaps even a fabrication or distortion of them. The Egyptian forces in Sinai were basically deployed in a defensive posture, caught totally by surprise during the Israeli preemptive strike on the morning of June 5, 1967. It seems highly unlikely that they had a concrete intention to launch a thorough attack against Israel. We tend therefore to adopt the claim that the message was probably designed to urge the leaders of Israel to order a pre-emptive strike against Egypt. This, as is well known now, was the demand of the IDF. An American refusal to accept the Israeli demands, which was almost certain, would most probably lead the government to authorize the IDF to launch a strike against Egypt.[31]

According to a State Department memo, American intelligence agencies discovered that Egypt had increased its order of battle in Sinai to approximately twenty thousand troops. However, the vast majority of those troops were located in the Suez Canal vicinity and not in offensive deployment near the border with Israel. A large force was concentrated in the Sharm el-Sheikh area – also a great distance from the Israeli–Egyptian border. According to the American assessment, the Egyptians had less than eight hundred tanks (the number that Israel gave) in Sinai. At this stage foreign forces had not entered Jordan. The Jordanian Chief-of-Staff, General Hamash, informed American officials that public statements bearing militant messages by Jordanian leaders on this issue were intended "for propaganda purposes", and should not, therefore, be taken too seriously.[32]

The memo further stated that Israel's claim that the visit to Moscow by the Egyptian Defense Minister, Shamas a-Din Badran, pointed to an Egyptian offensive, was unsubstantiated. Moreover, it was unlikely that Egypt would initiate a major military move when its defense minister was abroad. Israel also charged that four Egyptian missile boats which passed through the Suez Canal, heading south, had been ordered to reverse course and head north through the canal. By Israel's reckoning this too portended offensive activity. However, according to the American memo it more likely pointed to Egyptian fears of an impending Israeli strike, and perhaps an American one too.[33]

The memo mentioned the situation estimate that Israel had conveyed to the administration on May 22, two days before Eban's arrival in the United States. According to the Israeli account at this stage: (a) It would be suicidal for Egypt to try to invade Israel; (b) The Egyptian forces are gradually improving their strong defensive layout; (c) The Syrian forces are also in defense positions, and are therefore incapable of invading Israel; (d) The Jordanian and Lebanese armies do not pose a threat to Israel; and (e) Iraq is unable to contribute a significant number of forces to the war.[34]

Nevertheless, the memo referred to two incidents that might justify Israel's anxiety: (a) Units of Egypt's Fourth Armored Division had crossed the canal into Sinai; and (b) Egypt had pulled out armor, infantry, and air units from Yemen and transferred them to Sinai. Although these were steps that could galvanize Israeli fears, the memo determined that they could also be viewed as moves that Egypt had to make in the event of an Israeli attack.[35]

Given the severity and critical nature of the Israeli assessment that war was imminent, the head of the CIA, Richard Helms, ordered American intelligence bureaus to recheck their data and formulate an opinion on this issue. The president soon received a report that stated unequivocally that Israel's intelligence situation estimate was unreliable. It was most probably intended to squeeze aid from Washington, and perhaps justify an Israeli first strike. This was undoubtedly an accusation of unparalleled severity against Israel's intelligence community in one of the country's most critical periods. The following is the exact wording of the American report:

"We do not believe that the Israeli appreciation was a serious estimate of the sort they would submit to their own high officials. Rather, it is probably a gambit intended to influence the US to provide military supplies [to Israel], make more public commitments to Israel, approve Israeli military initiatives, and put more pressure on Egyptian President Nasser."[36]

Whatever the case, the categorical assurance of top administration officials regarding the defensive nature of Egypt's deployment in Sinai heightened the doubts gnawing at Eban regarding the credibility of the information contained in Eshkol's message to him. He probably regarded the message as an attempt by Israel's "military chiefs" to exploit the relatively convenient political circumstances – the fact that Eban was abroad on a diplomatic mission and the widespread public apprehension – in order to "take hold" of Eshkol's "mood" and views, and push him in the direction of a preventative strike. If indeed an Arab attack was imminent, as the message stated, and Washington, as expected, refused to consider it as an attack on the United States, then it was clear that Israel has no choice but to immediately launch a preemptive strike.

At the conclusion of the conversation with McNamara, Eban demonstratively expressed his disbelief in the information about an imminent Egyptian–Syrian attack, avowing that he was convinced the balance of forces had remained almost the same despite the recent realignments. He believed that Israel possessed military superiority and would emerge victorious on the battlefield. Nevertheless, even in optimum conditions it would pay an exorbitant price in human lives, and its cities would be vulnerable to massive bombing. Obviously, Washington could not remain neutral if hostilities erupted. If Eshkol demanded that the White House declare that "an attack on Israel would be considered an attack on the United States", then Israel would have to work out an improved form of deployment for the approaching clash.[37]

McNamara again gave no response; he felt under no obligation to answer Eban's requests when a person at the highest political level in Israel, at so crucial an hour, openly expressed skepticism in his country's Prime Minister and security branches. It was clear that Israel had to first "arrange affairs in its own house". Under these circumstances, McNamara could only end this disturbing conversation by assuring Eban that the president would clarify the administration's positions to him.[38]

At this point, Eban realized he was sliding into an unparalleled crisis of faith in American–Israeli relations that he was partially responsible for. As a last resort, which he believed might help to restore Israel's credibility, he made a special request to Eshkol: to receive details of the sources of Israel's intelligence estimate and to be allowed to present this information to the Americans. Only such clarifications, he implied, would dispel the administration's skepticism over the validity of the Prime Minister's message. "I cannot recommend strongly enough," Eban wrote to Eshkol, "that you ask [those responsible in the Israeli intelligence community] to permit [me] to tell them [the Americans] the nature of our sources. In addition to their wavering position on the crucial campaign, they are skeptical, or pretending to be skeptical, over the accuracy of the estimate."[39]

It is hard to conceive that Eban honestly believed Israel's intelligence branches would reveal the sources of the extremely sensitive information regarding Egypt's aggressive intentions to a foreign intelligence agency, even if it belonged to a superpower friendly to Israel. It is unclear whether Eban himself was aware of the nature of the "reliable sources" that Eshkol's message was based on. If he was then he could have safely assumed that his request to reveal the sources would be rejected. In this light, we may assume with a great degree of certainty that his unrealistic request was primarily intended to provide him with a strong "alibi" for his blatant unwillingness to adhere to the instructions in the prime minister's message. According to American sources, the intelligence branch handed Eban a "sample", whose nature and level of sensitivity regarding the estimate of an imminent attack is unclear.[40]

In effect, Eban realized from the very beginning of his mission in the US that he must lower the "message issue" as much as possible. Practically this meant that he would concentrate on the original goal of his mission – the closure of the Straits of Tiran to Israeli shipping, rather than on the danger of an immediate Egyptian–Syrian offensive and the demand that the American administration neutralize this danger, as requested by the prime minister.

Eban was not satisfied with this, as his talks with key administration officials revealed. He criticized the prime minister's message and its author, stressing that had he been in Israel at the time, such a message would never have been written. In this way he relayed to the American officials – and to the president in particular – in a most explicit manner that he did not take the prime minister's message seriously. In any case, his attitude towards the message clearly demonstrated to the administration that no significant meaning should be attributed to the message. If, despite all this, he brought it up in conversation, he would do so "out of necessity" because this was what his immediate superior, the prime minister, had instructed him to do.

It is hard to know whether Eban made this far-reaching decision to ignore the message alone; he may have consulted other ministers who saw eye to eye with him on these issues and who also wanted to avoid a military clash at almost any cost. First and foremost among them must have been the treasury minister, Pinchas Sapir. These men probably believed that the administration's rejection of Eshkol's demands, as they appeared in the message, would enhance the position of those who supported a hard line response to Egypt's provocations. In practice, this would almost certainly lead the way to the preemptive strike that they, the moderate ministers, wished to avoid. In addition to their strategic considerations, the moderate ministers also had fears of the internal political implications of a military course. They undoubtedly estimated that the decision for war would also produce dramatic changes in the fabric of the government, and strengthen the right-wing parties and Ben-Gurion's supporters. In fact, this is what happened when Moshe Dayan was appointed Defense Minister and Rafi (Ben-Gurion's party and the right-wing party, Gachal) entered the government. Be that as it may, Eban's handling of Israeli diplomacy in Washington exhibited the perilous phenomenon of a defective political culture within Israel at this period of time.

Regarding Egypt's closure of the Straits, Eban primarily sought to secure a promise, even if only vaguely-worded, of an American commitment to opening of the Straits. He tried to do this mainly by demonstrating that Israel really intended to launch a war in response to Nasser's belligerent moves, especially the blocking of the Straits. The only factor restraining Israel – and that would restrain it in the future – was the superpowers willingness to guarantee Israel freedom of navigation. Israel could not allow itself to wait much longer, and hoped to receive an immediate answer.

As noted, this line of thinking indicated that Eban and his staff were misreading the political map in the United States at this stage; our impression is that the Johnson Administration was fully informed of the prevalent mood among the Israeli leadership. During Eban's mission abroad, it was clear that the dominant position within the decision-makers in Israel still did not consider war a desirable option.

Consequently, Israel attempted to threaten a preventative strike if the Americans did not take its conditions seriously. In any case, as already pointed out, dominant circles in the administration were coming to the conclusion that a military confrontation was inevitable. Since the United States could not allow itself to take vigorous steps to guarantee Israel's navigational freedom through the Straits, the only realistic option was to let Israel act independently to secure its rights. In effect, there was no alternative. The US could only hope that it would not appear as the party that had consented to or encouraged Israel to strike first. Thus, Johnson and his advisors did not regard Eban's saber-rattling as a threat at all. Here too, we believe, Eban misjudged the reality of the unfolding events.

In a meeting with Under-Secretary of State Eugene Rostow, Eban described the "apocalyptic atmosphere" that pervaded the Israeli cabinet meeting of May 23 (following Nasser's announcement of the closure of the Straits of Tiran to Israeli vessels). According to Eban, Israel recognized the stark choice it faced: surrender or fight. But Ambassador Barbour's message offered Israel a third alternative for resolving the crisis: the possibility of international involvement that would guarantee freedom of navigation through the Straits. Eban made clear that Israel could be "convinced" to call off its military plans, providing that the maritime superpowers were willing to intervene concretely and ensure Israel's freedom of passage in the Red Sea.[41]

During the conversation Eban explained that 90 percent of Israel's imported oil came from Iran via the Straits. Thus, the closure of the Straits of Tiran would not only injure Israel's deterrent capability and strategic position, but would also strangle it economically – a tri-pronged disaster that Israel could not accept. Eban intimated that the army was pressing to execute a military operation, therefore the Israeli government had to convince both the army and the nation that they were justified in abstaining from war. And so, almost without realizing it, Eban depicted Israel and the United States as partners in the effort to restrain the IDF commanders who were itching to solve the crisis militarily. According to Eban, "a concrete alternative [was needed] which could give sufficient grounds for Israel not to launch an immediate preventative strike against Egypt".[42]

Eshkol's message was brought up during the conversation, as though accidentally. In this way Eban again managed to express his disinclination to follow the prime minister's instructions to present the message as a top priority. Rostow made it absolutely clear that no public announcement would be forthcoming in the spirit that Eshkol was asking for; that is, that an attack on Israel would be considered an attack on the US. To expect the president of the United States to make so sweeping a statement, he stressed, was naïve and unrealistic both politically and constitutionally. And, lest it be forgotten, the president was subordinate to constitutional procedures. Rostow's notes on his discussion with Eban revealed that the latter "was happy" to express complete understanding with Rostow's statements.[43]

Given Eban's status and the current circumstances, one would have expected that the Israeli Foreign Minister would "defend" his prime minister. Eban could have pleaded Eshkol's case as the noose around Israel's neck was tightening, and the Western superpowers, first and foremost the US, were not lifting a finger to extricate Israel from the danger. But Eban exhibited no tendency of this sort, instead saying that "he understands" the administration's predicament. Eban also expressed his realization that according to the United States' constitutional system the president could only commit himself to actions that were within the framework of official defense agreements. All that we are asking for, Eban pleaded, is an American commitment, as convincing as possible, regarding its intention to implement the naval operation plan.[44]

Then, in an attempt to demonstrate to Rostow that he too (Eban) was displeased with the prime minister's message, he claimed that "had he been in Tel Aviv he never would have worded the message this way". He emphasized that he (as opposed to those in Tel Aviv) was very familiar with the American constitutional system and was perfectly aware that the president could not take such a step. By taking this stand, Eban in effect cast aspersion on Eshkol, portraying his prime minister as an ignorant person who was not familiar with even the basic principles of the American government.[45]

Eban's words must have been satisfying to Rostow's ears. We may also assume that the under-secretary dashed off to convey the contents of his talk with the Israeli diplomat to the highest levels of government, firstly to Johnson. It is unclear what Eban's motive was for blatantly criticizing his government and the person who was trying to lead it through the crisis. Excluding the expression of a flawed political culture, a basic question must be asked here: What benefit did Eban think he would receive from the Americans for his criticism of his own government? A clear-cut answer to this question eludes us.[46]

At this stage the White House must have realized that it was dealing with a bungling and fractured Israeli government whose threshold of demands, as presented by the Foreign Minister, was relatively low and had nothing with which to pressure the administration. Thus, Rostow could satisfy Eban merely by sketching the principles of a plan that the administration was starting to formulate. Rostow explained that this plan would undergo several changes, according to comments and recommendations of various branches of the administration and an intensive examination by them.[47]

In simple language, the unhidden American message was that the implementation of the plan was a long way off. At a later stage it would have to be approved by UN institutions – another long and exhausting process whose "practical" results, from Israel's perspective, could by no means be guaranteed. Following this, an announcement would be made by the maritime states regarding the need to guarantee freedom of navigation through the Straits. Only in the final stage would a plan be formulated for the presence of an international flotilla in the region that, hopefully, would deter Egypt from interfering with international shipping freedom.[48]

Eban, an experienced diplomat, must have immediately understood that this was "a joke on the poor". He certainly knew that such a plan would make it virtually impossible to muzzle the "winds of war" blowing in Israel. He realized that he had no more realistic demands to make that could have been accepted by the administration, and therefore Eban chose the "middle path", entreating the American officials for concrete measures at the end of the process. Without "something pretty hard at the end of the road", as he defined it, he would be at a loss to convince his political colleagues to wait any longer. Intending to "put the fear of the devil" into Rostow, Eban informed him that there were many who felt that waiting would put Israel at grave risk.[49]

But, as Eban should have known, Rostow did not "fall off his chair" on hearing these war threats. On the contrary, he may have seen in them "a ray of light". Abba Eban was finally waking up to the fact that Israel could not expect the United States to do Israel's "dirty work", and instead must begin to think of a military solution to the crisis based on its own means. Naturally, the American Under Secretary did not wish to say these things straightforwardly. All that he could do was to express his commiseration with Eban's plight, while "impassively" accepting Eban's threats of Israeli preventative action. Be this as it may, from the way Rostow phrased his statement Eban could have assumed that the White House's plan for guaranteeing freedom of shipping in the Straits was still in its embryonic stage. Practically, this meant that it would be actualized, if ever, sometime in the distant future.[50]

Eban immediately expressed his disappointment at the American's intention to obtain the UN's approval for the plan. The time factor, he stressed, was of the utmost relevance for Israel at this period of time. Such a process, he justifiably averred, amounted to *ad nauseam* foot-dragging. He needed a "short cut". In practical terms, this meant an American declaration, in concert with other countries perhaps, of its intent to secure Israel's right to navigation in the Straits. Eban reckoned that no state would dare to challenge such an avowal, probably wanting to signal to Rostow that an American threat to use force would in itself be sufficient to reopen the Straits and convince Egypt to rethink its decision to block the waterway. In this way, Israel would get what it wanted without the United States having to risk heavy military involvement.[51]

Rostow wisely avoided responding to this proposal, whose implementation was likely to put the United States' credibility to the test. He was certainly aware of the fact that the proposal contained a high degree of risk for Washington. What if Egypt was not deterred by the threat and chose to stop American vessels in the Straits of Tiran by force? What would the US do in such a case? Would it restrain itself and suffer a severe blow to its prestige and deterrent capability? Or would it run the risk of sliding into a military confrontation with Egypt, and perhaps the Soviet Union as well? The White House had no interest in taking such a risk. Under these circumstances, Rostow seemed to have tried satisfying Eban, even if only slightly, by informing him that the administration had sent a warning to Egypt not to attack Israel. According to Rostow, "Eban seemed entirely satisfied", although Rostow did not show him the contents of the warning sent to Egypt.[52]

Available sources indicate that Washington's message to Egypt was primarily intended to divert Egypt from aggressive intentions towards Israel. This obviously had to be done in a highly sensitive manner. Rostow claimed that Egypt's "adversaries" (that is, Israel) believed that an Egyptian attack was imminent. The message stressed that Washington was not a party to these suspicions, and Rostow asserted that such a move was "unthinkable". The United States did not believe that Egypt would take such an irresponsible step, since it would have the gravest repercussions. It insisted, therefore, that Israel maintain its policy of restraint. Rostow defined the information regarding a possible imminent Egyptian attack on Israel as a "rumor", stressing that the United States "believed and hoped" it was not true. Thus, Egypt should mention it as a "friendly act".[53]

By the end of the conversation, Eban probably felt that Rostow had led him to think that the United States was sympathetic to Israel's fears. Practically, however, it refrained from granting Israel any solid commitment guaranteeing Israeli freedom of navigation in the Straits. What was more important – Eban was told with heavy innuendoes that the administration's plan of action, even if realized, was irrelevant for the immediate future. Eban in our view, "preferred to ignore" Rostow's not-so-discreet signals, pressing the under-secretary for specifics regarding the US proposal for a "plan of action". He wanted to know, for example, how long Israel should wait before sending a test vessel through the Straits. Eban seems to have naively believed here too that the threat of an Israeli test vessel through the Straits of Tiran would intimidate Rostow.[54]

But this track appeared only to have sparked Rostow's anger. He must have wondered how a diplomat as experienced and astute as Abba Eban "refused" to apprehend the signals the Americans were flashing him, urging Israel to quit begging for its life and begin taking the initiative to counter Egypt's aggressive moves. Rostow was left with little choice but to sharpen his message and present it more explicitly, in the hope that Eban would "pick up" the administration's intention. He told the Israeli Foreign Minister that the State Department "was recommending to the secretary a policy of not asking Israel to hold back any longer".[55]

It seemed that under the current circumstances, Washington could not express itself any more bluntly in giving Israel the green light to act as it saw fit. Despite this, Eban stubbornly refused "to swallow the bait", making it clear to Rostow that Israel would be satisfied with a protest and refrain from attacking if an arrangement could be reached with the United States. Rostow understood that "they would make protests but not strike, if an agreement could be attained on this approach".[56]

At the end of the talk, following refreshments, Rostow led Eban into a meeting with Secretary of State Dean Rusk. In his report to Eshkol, Eban stated that he maintained a tough and firm line. He told the Secretary of State that he had to leave the United States on May 27, in order to attend a government meeting the following day. In this way he implied that Israel was unwilling to enter exhausting and prolonged discussions on the postponement of an American decision. Eban also hinted that Israel would make a military move if the United States refused to live up to its word and guarantee freedom of shipping in the Straits. "Sunday's government meeting [May 28]," Eban told Rusk, "might be the most crucial meeting in the history of the State of Israel. Our decision [to go to war] will be determined by what the president tells me. U Thant is not a central player as far as we are concerned. I am speaking candidly when I say that in my opinion we will be in a war situation next week . . .

The only thing that might put off this decision is a declaration by the president that the United States has 'absolutely and unreservedly' decided to bring about the opening of the Straits to Israeli shipping."[57]

A very different impression of the Eban–Rusk talk appears in the Secretary of State's memo. Rusk's impression was that the meeting focused almost exclusively on the question of maritime freedom in the Straits, contrary to the Israeli Prime Minister's instructions. Moreover, Eban presented Israel's demands in a very "low key" manner, appearing to realize that he had no trump card left. All he hoped for was to return home with some kind of guarantee that would prevent his mission from being defined as a "colossal failure". He correctly judged that if he came back empty-handed Israel would be drawn much closer to the decision to go to war, and his own political standing would most probably be hurt.[58]

Eban appeared to have asked Rusk to give Israel "a ladder to climb down" from its bellicose stance without detracting too much from its prestige. "It's important," he told the secretary, that "I'll be able to say on my return to Tel Aviv that something concrete was done about the strait situation." According to Rusk's report, Eban refrained from making a concrete unconditional demand of the United States over the issue of maritime freedom. It is interesting to note that in the British Prime Minister's talks with Canadian leaders in early June 1967, Wilson pointed out that he himself was surprised that the only matter Eban demanded a guarantee for was the freedom of navigation in the Straits of Tiran.[59]

During his talk with Rusk, Eban lowered the threshold of his demands, stating that Israel was interested "in any possible action" connected with the Straits. He suggested that the president send a message to Eshkol, declaring that "we [the American administration] intend to open the Straits", and will proceed to discussions on the practical steps to be taken. Rusk avoided a definite response, noting that it was important to examine other alternatives. He summed up his opinion on the "moderateness" of Israel's demands, as Eban presented them, regarding the Straits issue in the following manner. "Eban emphasized," Rusk wrote, "that his government was interested **in any possible action** [my emphasis – Z.S.] related to the straits problem."[60]

Since embarking upon his mission only a few days earlier, Eban had certainly come a long way! He had consolidated his position on the crisis and the lessons Israel had to draw from the administration's handling of it. At first he had arrived with a sense of power, considering himself to be the fire and brimstone spokesman who supposedly had the "time bomb" that could force Washington to yield to Israel's main demands. He soon realized that all he had was a "cap gun" without any caps. Israel was facing one of the most critical moments in the crisis, and was totally unprepared for it. The situation demanded a decision, but the Israeli leadership, with Levi Eshkol at its head, lacked the necessary powers to reach a decision. Under these inauspicious circumstances Eban had had a rough landing on the tarmac of reality.

Suddenly the Secretary of State, not Eban, brought up the main issue in Eshkol's message; the danger of Egypt's troop concentrations in Sinai and the possibility of an Egyptian preemptive strike. Rusk noted that the president was not treating the prime minister's message "lightly". Nevertheless, American intelligence reports had not confirmed the Israeli message that a joint Egyptian–Syrian attack was imminent. Eban admitted that there were disturbing signs, such as the transfer of an Egyptian combat division from Yemen to Sinai, but this was a long-term matter. At present, the Egyptians were deployed defensively in Sinai, although this could change.[61]

Rusk also revealed that the UN Secretary-General, U Thant, was on his way to Egypt. In his view, it is very doubtful that the Egyptians would take such an extreme step (a military attack on Israel) that would be detrimental to the Secretary-General's prestige. Rusk further stressed that the president wanted Eban to understand that the White House could not accept Israel's request that it considers an attack on Israel in the same light as an attack on the United States. This could only become a real option if the president obtained congressional support. If Israel maintained its demand, Rusk warned that it would result in a painstakingly long debate in Congress. Thus, even before the administration knew about Eban's mission, the president had instructed the Secretary of State to obtain Congress's involvement in the crucial decisions in the crisis.[62]

As expected, Rusk had reservations about an Israeli strike, however he did not use his usual threatening tone if Israel decided to act otherwise. He simply stated that an Israeli preventive strike would cause the administration "extreme difficulty" (without revealing the nature of the difficulty). In the end, he offered Israel no alternative for handling the looming menace that it faced, other than the tepid suggestion to wait and see if the UN came up with a solution.[63]

The Secretary reported that Eban had brought up Eshkol's demands regarding the Egyptian military threat. According to Rusk's report, Eban made the prime minister's demand half-heartedly, as though reluctantly carrying out an order he had little faith in, and making explicit note of the fact that he "would not press this Israeli view and request". The Israeli Foreign Minister told his American counterpart that Prime Minister Eshkol "should not be held to specific language" with regard to his request of the president. Again Eban criticized Eshkol's message: "this telegram would not have been written as it was had [I] been there." Needless to say, as far as available sources shed light on the matter, Eban made no mention of these statements in his reports to the Prime Minister's Office.[64]

From Eban's handling of negotiations, Eshkol's reservations about assigning him this critical mission at this fateful hour become clear. Had Golda Meir been given the same task, as Eshkol wanted, she would have "shaken the hallowed corridors in Washington" and screamed "bloody murder" over the abandonment of Jewish people; so loud that no element in the administration would have been able to ignore her. Eban was of another cut – aloof, poised, and level-headed. Under ordinary circumstances, even in the case of a crisis – he was Israel's best man on the scene, but in late May 1967 he justified the apprehension that he was the wrong man for the task. Rusk's note at the end of his report that Eban had accepted his statements in a "relatively relaxed fashion" confirmed this view.[65]

Notes

1 Israeli–Syrian Relations

1 See State Department memorandum, talks between Secretary of State Dean Rusk and Syrian Foreign Minister Dr. Hassan Muraywid, December 19, 1964, *FRUS 1964–1968*, vol. XVII.
2 Avraham Sela, *Unity within Conflict in the Inter-Arab System: the Arab Summit Conferences, 1964–1982* (Jerusalem: Magnes Press, 1983), pp. 35–36 [Hebrew].
3 Ammar al-Sharif, "The People's Liberation War," Echoes and Responses: Excerpts from the Arab Press and Broadcasts, March 9, 1967, Dayan Center Archives, Tel Aviv University [Hebrew].
4 British Foreign Office memorandum, 1966 Survey of Syria, January 6, 1967, FCO 17/664, EY 1/1, 58952, Public Record Office [hereafter PRO].
5 State Department memorandum, February 23, 1966, *FRUS 1964–1968*, vol. XVII.
6 US embassy in Jordan report to the State Department, May 2, 1966, *FRUS 1964–1968*, vol. XVII.
7 Ibid.
8 US embassy in Israel report to the State Department, November 4, 1966, NND 959000, Box 2683, National Archives of the United States [hereafter NA].
9 See Zaki Shalom, *David Ben-Gurion, the State of Israel, and the Arab World, 1949–1956* (Brighton & Portland: Sussex Academic Press, 2002), pp. 4–6. See also, Edgar O'Ballance, *The Third Arab–Israeli War* (Connecticut: Faber and Faber, 1972), p. 20.
10 Eitan Haber, *The Day War Broke Out* (Tel Aviv: Yidanim, 1987), pp. 95–96 [Hebrew] [hereafter Haber, *The Day War Broke Out*].

2 Israel and the Hashemite Kingdom

1 See in this regard Avi Shlaim, *Collusion across the Jordan: King Abdullah, the Zionist Movement, and the Partition of Palestine* (Columbia University Press, 1988).
2 On the 1955–1957 crisis see Uriel Dan, *King Hussein and the Challenge of Arab Radicalism, Jordan 1955–1957* (New York: Oxford University Press, 1989), pp. 21–77.

3 See Asher Susser, *Jordan, Case Study of a Pivotal State* (Washington DC: The Washington Institute for Near East Policy, 2000), pp. 14–16.

4 On Western assistance to Jordan in the 1958 crisis, see Michael Oren, "The Test of Suez: Israel and the Middle East Crisis of 1958," *Studies in Zionism*, 12 (1991), pp. 55–84.

5 Prime Minister report, David Ben-Gurion on his talks with UN Secretary Dag Hammarskjöld, Israel Government Protocol, January 4, 1959, Notes from the Eighth Government Session, 1959, vol. XIX, pp. 10–11 [Hebrew].

6 Protocol from the government session, August 10, 1958, Notes from the Eighth Government Session, vol. XII, p. 18.

7 On the tension in Jordanian–Syrian relations prior to the Six Day War see British Embassy in Damascus report to the British Foreign Office, February 6, 1967, FCO 17/231, PRO.

8 United States Embassy in Jordan report to the US State Department, April 24, 1966, Under-Secretary of State Hare with King Hussein, *FRUS 1964–1968*, vol. XVII. See the internet site: <http://www.state.gov/www/about_state/history/vol_xviii/zc.html>.

9 Ibid.

3 The Samu Raid – Background and Outcome

1 British embassy in Israel report to British Foreign Office, December 21, 1966, FO 371/186840, PRO.

2 Ibid.

3 Ibid.

4 Ibid.

5 Ibid.

6 United States Embassy in Israel report to State Department, March 29, 1967, NND 969000, Box 29, NA. See also: Avi Shlaim, "An Interview with Yitzhak Rabin, Tel Aviv, August 22, 1982," *Iyunim Bitikumat Israel*, 8 (1998) [Hebrew].

7 Haber, *The Day War Broke Out*, pp. 108–109.

8 Ibid.

9 British embassy in Israel report to British Foreign Office, December 21, 1966, FO 371/186840, PRO.

10 Prime Minister's Office memorandum, November 13, 1967, Division 15, Galili, File 2, Carton 87, Kibbutz Meuchad Archives, Yad Tabenkin, Ramat Efal [hereafter: KMA].

11 Ibid.

12 Prime Minister's Office memorandum, December 15, 1966, 7227/10/A, Israel State Archives [hereafter; ISA].

13 Canadian Embassy in Egypt Report to Canadian Foreign Office,

December 2, 1966, RG 25, vol. 8885, FILE – 20 UAR-1-3 PL.7, NAC.

14 Zeev Bar-Lavi, "The Hashemite Regime 1949–1967 and its Standing in the West Bank," Shiloah Institute for Middle East Research (Tel Aviv: Shiloah, 1981), p. 45 [Hebrew].

15 Ibid. See also: Adnan Abu-Odeh, *Jordanians, Palestinians & The Hashemite Kingdom in the Middle East Peace Process* (Washington: United States Institute of Peace Press, 1999), pp. 130–132.

16 British Foreign Office memorandum, December 10, 1966, FO 371/186840, PRO. On the raid's impact on Jordan, see Asher Susser, *On Both Banks of the Jordan: A Political Biography of Wasfi al-Tal* (London: Frank Cass, 1994), pp. 110–116.

17 British Foreign Office memorandum, December 10, 1966, FO 371/186840, PRO.

18 See Avi Shlaim, "His Royal Shyness, King Hussein and Israel," *The New York Review* (July 15, 1999), p. 15.

19 Ibid.

20 Ibid.

21 Ibid.

22 Ibid.

23 Asher Susser, "Jordan and the Six Day War," in Asher Susser (ed.), *Six Days – Thirty Years: A New Look at the Six Day War* (Tel Aviv: Am Oved, 1999), p. 106 [Hebrew].

24 British Foreign Office memorandum, November 14, 1966, FO 371/186839, PRO.

25 Ibid.

26 Israeli embassy in the United States report to Israeli Foreign Ministry, November 21, 1966, FM 4030/7, ISA.

27 Ibid.

28 Ibid.

29 State Department memorandum to US embassy in Israel, November 13, 1966, *FRUS 1964–1968*, vol. XVIII. See the internet site: <http://www.state.gov/www/about_state/history/vol_xviii/index html>.

30 Prime Minister's Office memorandum, no date available, 7337/43/A, ISA.

31 Prime Minister's Office memorandum, November 13, 1966, Division 15, File 4, Box 87, KMA.

32 Ibid.

33 State Department memorandum to the US embassy in Israel, November 13, 1966, *FRUS 1964–1968*, vol. XVIII. See the internet site: <http://www.state.gov/www/about_state/history/vol_xviii/ index. html>.

See also: British embassy in Israel report to British Foreign Office, November 14, 1966, FO 371/186838 PRO. On Odd Bull's mission in the Middle East see Odd Bull, *War and Peace in the Middle East: The Experiences and Views of a UN Observer* (London: Cooper, 1976).

34 State Department memorandum, March 21, 1967, NSF, Country File, Israel, Vol. 6, Box 140, Lyndon Johnson Library [hereafter: LJL].

35 Ibid.

36 Prime Minister's Office memorandum, December 15, 1966, 7227.10/A, ISA.

37 Israeli embassy in the United States report to Israeli Foreign Ministry, November 16, 1966, FM 403/6, ISA. On the Samu operation and its results see also Samir A. Mutawi, *Jordan in the 1967 War* (London: Cambridge University Press, 1987), pp. 76–84.

38 State Department memorandum, conversation between US secretary of state and Israeli ambassador to the United States, and the Israeli Prime Minister's message to President Johnson, November 21, 1966, NND 959000, NA.

39 Ibid.

40 Prime Minister's Office memorandum, Instructions to Ambassador Harman, no date, 7230/21/A, ISA.

41 Ibid.

42 White House memorandum, November 24, 1966, NSF, Country File Israel, Volume 6, Box 140, LJL.

43 Ibid.

44 On King Hussein's criticism of the United States, see Israeli Foreign Ministry report to Israeli embassy in the United States, November 16, 1966, 4030/6/FM, ISA. On the president's message, see State Department memorandum, November 23, 1966, NND 959000 NA.

45 White House memorandum, November 24, 1966, NSF, Country File Israel, Volume 6, Box 140, LJL.

46 United States embassy in Jordan report to US State Department, December 11, 1966, *FRUS 1964–1968*. See the internet site: <http://www.state.gov/www/about_state/history/vol_xviii/index.html>.

47 Ibid.

48 Ibid.

49 Ibid.

50 Ibid.

51 Meeting of Rafi, May 21, 1967, LMA, Beit Berl.

52 Ibid.

53 Foreign Ministry memorandum, January 9, 1967, 4092/14 FM, ISA.

54 Prime Minister's Office memorandum, December 15, 1966, 7227/10/A, ISA.

4 Israel, Syria and the Policy of Escalation

1 Yoel Nir, "Incidents in the North," *Mabat Chadash, Shavuon Midini* (August 3, 1966), p. 12 [Hebrew].

2 For Chief-of-Staff Rabin's statements on August 22, 1967, see Yemima Rosental (ed.), *Yitzhak Rabin, Prime Minister of Israel – 1974–1977, 1992–1995, Selected Documents from his Life, Volume I, 1922–1967* (Jerusalem: Israel State Archives, 2005), pp. 412–413 [hereafter: Rosental: *Rabin*].

3 Matatitu Meisel, "The Battle on the Golan, June 1967," *Maarachot* (2001), p. 25 [hereafter: Meisel, "Battle on the Golan"].

4 Several days prior to the Sinai Campaign, Ben-Gurion noted in his diary: "My plan includes . . . overthrowing Nasser (if possible), dividing Jordan – the eastern [part will go] to Iraq [the western part to Israel], slicing up Lebanon's territory in order to set up a Christian state." See: *Ben-Gurion Diary,* October 22, 1956, Ben-Gurion Archives [hereafter: BGA].

5 Meisel, "Battle on the Golan," p. 25.

6 Ibid.

7 Ibid.

8 Haber, *The Day War Broke Out*, p. 146.

9 Ibid.

10 Ami Gloska, "The Showdown between the General Staff and the Eshkol Government in the 'Waiting Period' – May–June 1967," *Leonard Davis School of International Relations,* Publication No. 88 (June 2001), p. 10.

11 State Department memorandum, October 27, 1966, NND 959000, Box 2768, NA.

12 Lecture by Yosi Olmert, "A Professional Day on the Six-Day War," February 3, 1987, pp. 11–12, KMA.

13 Lecture by Shlomo Gazit, "Seminar on the Results of the Six-Day War as a Political Challenge for Israel," Tel Aviv University, Dayan Center for Middle Eastern and African Studies, March 5, 1986, pp. 3–4.

14 Intelligence Branch memorandum, "The Syrian–Egyptian Defense Pact – An Evaluation," November 4, 1966, Hertz 4096/2, 1966, ISA. See also: Moshe Shemesh, *From the Nakba to the Nachsa: The Arab–Israeli Conflict and the Palestinian National Problem 1957–1967, Nasser's Road to the Six-Day War* (Sde Boker: Ben-Gurion Institute, 2004), pp. 570–572.

15 Intelligence Branch memorandum, "The Syrian–Egyptian Defense Pact – An Evaluation," November 4, 1966, hetz 4096/2, 1966, ISA.

16 Report from the Israeli embassy in the United States to Israel Foreign Ministry, January 26, 1965, hetz 6553/19, ISA.

17 Ibid.

18 State Department memorandum, January 16, 1967, *FRUS 1964–1968*, vol. XVII

19 Report from US embassy in Israel to State Department, February 8, 1965, NND 959000, Box 1650, NA.

20 Ibid.

21 Ibid.

22 Report from British embassy in Syria to British Foreign Ministry, conversation between British ambassador in Syria and Syrian Foreign Minister, Ibrahim Machus, January 8, 1966, FCO 17/473, 58903, PRO.

23 Ibid.

24 Ibid.

25 State Department memorandum, January 16, 1967, *FRUS 1964–1968*, vol. XVII.

26 Ibid.

27 State Department memorandum, January 17, 1967, *FRUS 1964–1968*, vol. XVII.

28 Ibid.

29 Ibid.

30 Ibid.

31 See *Daily Report*, January 3, 1967, No. 1, 1967, Dayan Center Archives, Tel Aviv University.

32 Ibid.

33 Israeli Foreign Ministry report to Israeli embassy in the United States, February 16, 1967, hetz 3975/17, ISA.

34 Ibid.

35 Israeli Foreign Ministry report to Israeli embassy in the United States, March 19, 1967, hetz 3975/17, ISA.

36 Ibid.

37 British embassy in Israel report to British Foreign Ministry, March 16, 1967, E/2, PRO.

38 Israeli Foreign Ministry report to Israeli embassy in the United States, March 31, 1967, hetz 3975/17, ISA.

39 Ibid.

40 British Foreign Ministry memorandum, April 11, 1967, FCO 17/473, 58903, PRO.

41 Ibid.

42 Ibid.

43 On Yariv's meeting with military attaches, see British embassy in Israel report to British Foreign Ministry, April 14, 1967, FCO 17/473, 58903, PRO.

44 Ibid.

45 Ibid.

46 Ibid.

47 Ibid.
48 Ibid.
49 Ibid.
50 Ibid.
51 Ibid.
52 Ibid.
53 Ibid.
54 On the statements made by Chief-of-Staff Yitzhak Rabin in the general staff meeting, April 24, 1967, see Rosental, *Rabin*, pp. 438–439.
55 State Department memorandum, May 10, 1967, in FCO 17/473, 58903, PRO. See also NSF, NCS, History, Middle East Crisis, May 12–June 19, 1967, Vol. 9, Container 20, pp. 6–7, LJL [hereafter: State Department Documents, May–June 1967 Crisis, Vol. I].
56 See Meeting between the United States ambassador in Syria with Syrian Foreign Minister, Dr. Adis Daudi, May 13, 1967, State Department memorandum, May 13 in State Department Documents, May–June 1967 Crisis, Vol. I, p. 9.
57 Ibid.
58 United States embassy in Israel report to State Department, May 9, 1967, NND 969000, Box 2184, NA.
59 State Department memorandum, May 12, 1967, *FRUS 1964–1968*, vol. XVII.
60 Ibid.
61 Ibid.
62 Ibid.
63 Foreign Ministry memorandum, April 12, 1967, hetz 4046/2, ISA. On the dispute in the American administration between supporters and opponents of Israel, see Avi Shlaim, *War and Peace in the Middle East: a Concise History* (New York: Penguin Books, 1995), pp. 38–40.
64 Ibid.
65 Israeli Foreign Ministry report to Israeli embassy in the United States, May 12, 1967, Rabin Center Archives.
66 Ibid.
67 Ami Gloska, *Eshkol: Give an Order: The IDF and the Israel Government on the Way to the Six-Day War, 1963–1967* (Tel Aviv: Maarekhot, 2004), p. 192 [Hebrew].
68 On Dayan's conduct under similar circumstances see: Moshe Dayan, *Milestones, An Autobiography* (Jerusalem: Idanim Publishers, 1967), p. 151.
69 On the moderate responses of Syria following the April, 1967 incident, see British embassy in Syria report to British Foreign Ministry, April 27, 1967, FCO 17/665, 58952, EY 1/2, PRO.

5 The Beginning of the Crisis – Perception of the Threat

1 United States embassy in Syria report to State Department, April 11 and 28, 1967, NND 969000, Box 2486, NA.

2 United States embassy in Syria report to State Department, May 21 and 23, 1967, NND 969000, Box 1795, NA.

3 State Department memorandum, May 12, 1967, NND 969000, Box 2185, NA.

4 IDF GHQ/Training Dept History, *The Six Day WAR* – The Campaign in the Egyptian Theater, December 1971, p. 83 [hereafter: GHQ/Training Dept, Egyptian Theater] [Hebrew]. See also, Yosi Goldstein, *Eshkol, A Biography* (Tel Aviv: Keter Publishing House, 2003), pp. 539–540 [Hebrew].

5 Major Yona, "The Background to the Six Day War in Arab Eyes,"*Ma'arachot*, 191–192 (June 1968), pp. 37–40 [Hebrew].

6 CIA memorandum, June 19, 1967, NSF, Country File Middle East Crisis, Vol. 6, Box 109, LJL. On the evacuation of UN forces from Sinai, see Mahmoud Riad, *The struggle for Peace in the Middle East* (London: Quartet Books, 1981), pp. 18–19.

7 CIA memorandum, June 19, 1967, NSF, Country File Middle East Crisis, Vol. 6, Box 109, LJL.

8 GHQ/Training Dept, Egyptian Theater, pp. 41–42. On the characteristics of the UN Emergency Force (UNEF) and its legal status see CIA memorandum, May 17, 1967, *FRUS 1964–1968*, Vol. XIX.

9 State Department memorandum, May 19, 1967, NND 969000, Box 1796, NA. See also Michael Oren, *Six Days of War: The Campaign that Changed the Face of the Middle East* (Tel Aviv: Dvir Publishers, 2004), pp. 93–95 [Hebrew].

10 See: CIA memorandum, June 19, 1967, NSF, Country File Middle East Crisis, Vol. 6, Box 109, LJL

11 Ibid.

12 Ibid.

13 On the Nasser-Montgomery meeting see British embassy in Egypt report to the British Foreign Office, May 17, 1967, FCO 39/265, VK 3/16, P.R.O. On the Nasser-Anderson conversation see: United States embassy in Portugal report to State Department, June 2, 1967, NND 969000, Box 1795, NA.

14 CIA memorandum, May 26, 1967, see also State Department memorandum, May 25, 1967, NSF, Country File Middle East Crisis, Vol. 2, Box 106, LJL. On the conspiracy theory, see Elie Podeh, "The Lie that Won't Die: Collusion 1967," *Middle East Quarterly*, Vol. XI, No. 1 (2004), pp. 51–62.

15 State Department memorandum, The President in the Middle East Crisis, May 12–June 19, 1967, December 19, 1968, NSF, NSC

Histories, The Middle East Crisis, Vol. 1, Tabs 1–10, No. 2, LJL. On the information that Soviet Union conveyed to Egypt dealing with Israel's intentions to attack Syria, see Mohamed Heikal, *The Sphinx and the Commissar: The Rise and Fall of Soviet Influence in the Middle East* (New York: Harper & Row, 1978), pp. 172–180.

16 United States embassy in Egypt report to State Department, May 21, 1967, NND 969000, Box 1795, NA.

17 United States ambassador in Egypt conversation with Egyptian Foreign Minister, Mahmoud Riad, United States embassy in Egypt report to State Department, May 23, 1967, NND 969000, Box 1795, NA.

18 United States embassy in Egypt report to the State Department, March 5, 1967, NND 969000, Box 2490, NA.

19 Ibid.

20 United States ambassador in Egypt conversation with the Egyptian Foreign Minister, Mahmoud Riad, United States embassy in Egypt report to State Department, May 23, 1967, NND 969000, Box 1795, NA.

21 Ibid.

22 State Department memorandum, conversation of the president's advisor, Walt Rostow, May 31, 1967, *FRUS, 1964–1968*, Vol. XIX.

23 Ibid.

24 State Department memorandum, May 28 and 31, 1967, NND 969000, Box 1793, NA.

25 President Nasser's conversation with the UN Secretary-General, U Thant, United States embassy in Egypt report to State Department, May 26, 1967, NND 969000, Box 1795, NA.

26 Ibid.

27 Ibid.

28 Abba Eban, *Life's Chapters*, Vol. 2 (Tel Aviv: Ma'ariv Publishers, 1978), p. 359–360 [hereafter: Eban, *Life's Chapters*] [in Hebrew].

29 Special Intelligence Review, "The Egyptians' Situation Estimate May 1967," GHQ, Intelligence Branch, August 16, 1967, General File, BGA.

30 Ibid.

31 Moshe Shai, "The Chief-of-Staff: One Punitive Operation was Insufficient for the Syrians," no date, Division (hativa) 15, Galili, File 1–2, Container 94, KMA.

32 State Department memorandum, May 18, 1967, NND 969000, Box 2490, NA.

33 Lecture by Aharon Yariv at the Moshe Dayan Center, Tel Aviv University, "Twenty Years," pp. 7–8.

34 Aryeh Baron, *Personal Signature: Moshe Dayan in the Six Day WAR* (Tel Aviv: Yediot Achronot Publishers, 1997), p. 17 [Hebrew].

35 GHQ/Training Dept, The Egyptian Theater, pp. 41–42.
36 Discussion in the IDF's GHQ, May 16/17, 1967.
37 United States embassy in Israel report to State Department, May 18, 1967, NND 969000, Box 1796, NA.
38 State Department memorandum, The President in the Middle East Crisis, May 12–June 19, 1967, December 19, 1968, NSF, NSC Histories, The Middle East Crisis, Vol. 1, Tabs 1–10, No. 2, LJL.
39 Israeli Foreign Ministry report to the Israeli ambassador in the UN, May 15, 1967, and also, Israeli embassy in the UN report to the Foreign Ministry, May 16, 1967, File 7920/1 A, ISA.
40 Israeli Foreign Ministry report to the Israeli Delegation in the UN, May 21, 1967, File 7920/1 A, ISA.
41 United States Delegation to the UN report to the State Department, May 19, 1967, NND 969000, Box 1796, NA.
42 Israeli Foreign Ministry report to the Israeli ambassador to the U.N, May 17, 1967, and also, Israeli Embassy in the U.N report to the Foreign Ministry, May 17, 1967, File 7920/1 A, ISA.
43 The United States Delegation to the U.N report to the State Department, May 18, 1967, NND 969000, Box 1796, NA.
44 State Department memorandum, May 15, 1967, NND 969000, Box 1796, NA.
45 United States embassy in Egypt report to State Department, May 16, 1967, *FRUS, 1964–1968*, Vol. XIX.
46 State Department memorandum, May 17, 1967, NND 969000, Box 2185, NA.
47 Ibid.
48 On the administration's guarantees to Israel, see State Department memorandum, May 23, 1967, NND 969000, Box 1795, NA.
49 Efraim Evron lecture, Dayan Center, "The American Theater," p. 8.
50 Eban–Barbour conversation, United States Embassy in Israel report to the State Department, May 18, 1967, NND 969000, Box 1795, NA.
51 State Department memorandum, May 18, 1967, NND 969000, Box 1796, NA.
52 Hal Saunders wrote the memorandum. See: State Department memorandum, December 20, 1968, NSF, NSC Histories, The Middle East Crisis, Vol. 1, Tabs 1–10, No. 2, LJL.
53 Ibid.
54 See Prime Minister Eshkol's message to President Johnson, May 18, 1967, NND 969000, Box 1816, NA. Secretary also: United States embassy in Israel report to the State Department, May 18, 1967, *FRUS, 1964–1968*, Vol. XIX.
55 Ibid.
56 Ibid.

57 State Department memorandum, May 18, 1967, NND 969000, Box 1795, NA.

58 Ibid.

59 Ibid.

60 Ibid.

61 Ibid.

62 Ibid.

63 See Ambassador Harman's conversation with Under-Secretary of State Eugene Rostow, State Department memorandum, May 17, 1967, NND 969000, Box 1796, NA.

64 Ibid.

65 United States embassy in Israel report to State Department, May 18, 1967, NND 969000, Box 1795, NA.

66 Ibid.

67 Prime Minister's Office report, May 18, 1967, File 7920/4 A, ISA.

68 Ibid.

6 Dramatic Change in the Perception of the Threat

1 Prime Minister's Office report, May 18, 1967, File 7920/4 A, ISA.

2 State Department memorandum, May 18, 1967, NND 969000, Box 1796, NA.

3 United States embassy in Israel report to State Department, May 18, 1967, NND 969000, Box 1795, NA.

4 Ibid.

5 Ibid.

6 State Department report to United States embassy in the Soviet Union, May 18, 1967, in: State Department Documents, *May–June 1967 Crisis*, Vol. 1, p. 16.

7 State Department memorandum, May 18, 1967, in: State Department Documents, *May–June 1967 Crisis*, Vol. 1, p. 17.

8 Ibid.

9 United States embassy in Israel report to the State Department, May 19, 1967, NND 969000, Box 1796, NA.

10 Ibid.

11 Haber, *The Day that War Broke Out*, p. 62.

12 IDF GHQ discussion, 17/67, May 19, 1967, Rabin Center Archives.

13 United States embassy in Israel report to State Department, May 19, 1967, NND 969000, Box 1818, NA.

14 Ibid.

15 Ibid.

16 Ibid.

17 Ibid.

18 Statements made by Chief-of-Staff Yitzhak Rabin in the GHQ meeting, May 19, 1967, in: Rosental, *Rabin*, p. 448 [Hebrew].

19 A State Department memorandum determined that there was solid proof that the Egyptians had used poison gas in North Yemen. State Department memorandum, May 20, 1967, NND 969000, Box 2487, NA.

20 Eugene Rostow's memorandum to Secretary of State, May 20, 1967, NND 989509, Box 15, NA.

21 Ibid.

22 Eban's original version in English: "Israel had been disturbed because it had not sensed from the US the kind of identification, the kind of special support it had hoped to receive." United States embassy in Israel report to the State Department, May 21, 1967, NND 969000, Box 1795, NA.

23 Ibid.

24 Ibid.

25 State Department memorandum, May 31, 1967, NSF, Country File Middle East Crisis, Vol. 3, Box 107, LJL.

26 United States embassy in Israel report to the State Department, May 21, 1967, NND 969000, Box 1795, NA.

27 Ibid.

28 Ibid. in State Department Documents, *May–June 1967 Crisis*, Vol. 1, pp. 25–26. See also: United States in Israel report to the State Department, May 21, 1967, NND 969000, Box 1795, NA.

29 Ibid.

30 Ibid.

31 United States embassy in Syria report to the State Department, May 20, 1967, *FRUS 1964–1968*, Vol. XIX.

32 Ibid.

33 Israeli Foreign Minister report to Israeli Ambassador in the U.N, May 21, 1967, File 7920/1 A, ISA.

34 Ibid.

35 State Department memorandum, May 21, 1967, NND 969000 Box 1795, NA.

36 Ibid.

37 Ibid.

38 State Department memorandum, May 22, 1967, NND 969000, Box 1795, NA.

39 Ibid.

40 Ibid.

41 Ibid.

42 Ibid.

43 State Department memorandum, May 23, 1967, NND 969000, Box 1795, NA.

44 State Department memorandum, June 2, 1967, NND 969000, Box 1795, NA.

45 State Department report to United States embassy in Egypt, May 22, 1967, *FRUS 1964–1968*, Vol. XIX.
46 Ibid.
47 Ibid.
48 United States embassy in Israel report to the State Department, May 21, 1967, in: State Department Documents, *May–June 1967 Crisis*, Vol. 1, p. 29.
49 Ibid.

7 Blocking the Straits of Tiran

1 State Department memorandum, May 23, 1967, *FRUS 1964–1968*, Vol. XIX.
2 Ibid.
3 State Department report to the United States embassy in the Soviet Union, May 23, 1967, *FRUS 1964–1968*, Vol. XIX.
4 State Department report to the United States embassy in the Soviet Union, May 23, 1967, *FRUS 1964–1968*, Vol. XIX.
5 Ibid.
6 State Department memorandum to the United States ambassador in Egypt, May 22, 1967, in: State Department Documents, *May–June 1967 Crisis*, Vol. 1, p. 32.
7 Ibid.
8 United States embassy in Egypt report to the State Department, May 23, 1967, in: State Department Documents, *May–June 1967 Crisis*, Vol. 1, p. 32.
9 Ibid.
10 State Department report to the United States embassy in Israel, May 23, 1967, in: State Department Documents, *May–June 1967 Crisis*, Vol. 1, p. 34.
11 Ibid.
12 Ibid.
13 Ibid.
14 Ibid.
15 Efraim Evron lecture, Dayan Center, "The American Theater," p. 15.
16 State Department report to the United States embassy in Britain, May 23, 1967, in: in State Department Documents, *May–June 1967 Crisis*, Vol. 1, pp. 35–36.
17 Ibid.
18 From the discussion in the British Cabinet it turns out that the prime minister expressed vigorous opposition to Britain standing alone as the leader in the struggle for guaranteeing freedom of passage through the straits. British Foreign Office memorandum, May 28, 1967, PREM 13/1618, 53650, P.R.O.

19 Ibid.
20 White House memorandum, May 23, 1967, in: State Department Documents, *May–June 1967 Crisis*, Vol. 1, p. 37.
21 State Department memorandum, May 24, 1967, in: State Department Documents, *May–June 1967 Crisis*, Vol. 1, pp. 44–45.
22 Ibid., pp. 46–47.
23 Ibid., p. 50.
24 Ibid.
25 Ibid.

8 Abba Eban's Mission: Phase I

1 Discussion in the GHQ and government meeting, May 23, 1967, in Rosental, *Rabin*, pp. 456–457.
2 Ibid.
3 Michael Oren, "Six Days of War: The Campaign that Changed the Face of the Middle East," *Dvir* (2004), p. 116.
4 Report from the United States embassy in Israel to the State Department, May 23, 1967, NND 969000, Box 1795, NA.
The following is the exact wording of the British proposal:
'We propose to study urgently, in consultation with the Americans, the question of action, in collaboration with other maritime countries concerned with access to the Gulf of Aqaba.'
Report from the British embassy in Israel to the British Foreign Office, May 23, 1967, FCO 17/483, 58902, P.R.O.
5 Ibid.
6 See the Chief-of-Staff's statements, Yitzhak Rabin in the government session of May 23, 1967, in Rosental, *Rabin*, pp. 457–458.
7 Ibid.
8 Eban, *Life's Chapters*, pp. 328–330.
9 Haber, *The Day that War Broke Out*, p. 170. See also, Eban, *Life's Chapters*, p. 333.
10 Report from the Israeli embassy in the United States to the Foreign Ministry, May 23, 1967, hetz 5937/30, Israel State Archive [hereafter: ISA].
11 Ibid.
12 Michael Bar-Zohar, *The Longest Month* (Tel Aviv: Leon Epstein, 1968), p. 96 [Hebrew].
13 Ibid.
14 Ibid.
15 Ibid.
16 See State Department memorandum, Editor's Note, May 23, 1967, *FRUS 1964–1968*, Vol. XIX.
17 Ibid.

18 State Department memorandum, May 24, 1967, NSF, NSC, History, Middle East Crisis, Vol. 4, Box 2, LJL. See also Protocol of the National Security Council Meeting, May 24, 1967, FRUS 1964–1968, Vol. XIX.

19 Ibid.

20 Ibid.

21 Ibid.

22 Ibid.

23 Ibid.

24 Ibid.

25 Ibid.

26 Ibid.

27 Ibid.

28 Ibid.

29 Ibid.

30 Ibid.

31 Ibid.

32 Report from the United States embassy in France to the State Department, May 23, 1967, in State Department Files, The May–June Crisis 1967, Vol. I, p. 39–40.

33 Ibid.

34 Report from the Israeli embassy in France to the Israeli Foreign Ministry, May 24, 1967, hetz 4084/2, ISA.

35 Ibid.

36 Ibid.

37 Abba Eban, *An Autobiography* (New York: Random House, 1977), p. 337.

38 Report from the Israeli delegation in New York to the Foreign Ministry, May 2, 1967, hetz 4078/7, ISA. See also the report from the Israeli embassy in France to the Israeli Foreign Ministry, May 27, 1967, hetz 4084/2, ISA.

39 Report from the Israeli embassy in France to the Israeli Foreign Ministry, June 3, 1967, hetz 5937/30, ISA.

40 Ibid.

41 Ibid.

42 Ibid.

43 Report from the Israeli embassy in Britain to the Israeli Foreign Ministry, May 23 and 24, 1967, File 7920/1 A, ISA. See also British Foreign Ministry memo, Eban–Wilson Conversation, May 24, 1967, FCO 17/483, 58902, P.R.O.

44 Ibid.

45 Ibid.

46 Ibid.

47 Ibid.

9 Abba Eban's Mission: Phase II

1 State Department memorandum, May 25, 1867, NND 969000, Box 1795, NA. See also William Quandt, "Lyndon Johnson, the Middle East and the 1967 War: What Color was the Light?" *Middle East Journal*, Vol. 46, No. 2 (1993), p. 208.

2 Ibid.

3 Abba Eban, *Personal Witness: Israel Through my Eyes* (London: Jonathan Cape Ltd., 1993), p. 382 [hereafter, Eban, *Personal Witness*].

4 Ibid.

5 Eban, *Life's Chapter*, pp. 344–345.

6 Eban, *Personal Witness*, p. 382.

7 United States embassy in Israel report to the State Department, May 24, 1967, NND 969000, Box 1795, NA.

8 Ibid.

9 Ibid.

10 Defense Department memorandum, Conversation between the Secretary of Defense and Abba Eban, May 26, 1967, NSF, NSC Histories, Middle East Crisis, May 12–June 19, 1967, Tabs 31–42, Box 17, LJL.

11 Ibid.

12 Ibid.

13 Ibid.

14 Ibid.

15 Ibid.

16 Ibid.

17 Ibid.

18 Ibid.

19 Ibid.

20 Ibid.

21 Ibid.

22 Ibid.

23 Ibid.

24 Ibid.

25 Ibid.

26 Ibid.

27 Ibid.

28 Ibid.

29 Ibid.

30 Ibid.

31 State Department memorandum, Research and Intelligence Unit, May 26, 1967, NSF, Country File, Middle East Crisis, Vol. 2, Box. 105, LJL.

32 Ibid.

33 Ibid.

34 Ibid.
35 Ibid.
36 Ibid.
37 Defense Department memorandum, Conversation between the Secretary of Defense and Abba Eban, May 26, 1967, NSF, NSC Histories, Middle East Crisis, May 12–June 19, 1967, Tabs 31–42, Box 17, LJL.
38 Ibid.
39 Foreign Minister's report to the Prime Minister's Office, May 26, 1967, hetz 5937/30, ISA.
40 State Department memorandum, May 25, 1967, NND 989509, Box 19, NA.
41 State Department memorandum, May 25, 1967, NND 969000, Box 2185, NA.
42 Ibid.
43 Ibid.
44 State Department memorandum, May 26, 1967, NND 969000, Box 1795, NA.
45 Ibid.
46 Ibid.
47 Ibid.
48 Ibid.
49 Ibid.
50 Ibid.
51 Ibid.
52 Ibid.
53 Ibid.
54 State Department memorandum, May 25, 1967, NND 989509, Box 19, NA.
55 Ibid.
56 Ibid.
57 Israeli embassy in the United States report to the Israeli Foreign Ministry, May 26, 1967, hetz 5937/30, ISA. On the Eban–Rusk talk, see also State Department memo, May 25, 1967, *FRUS, 1964–1968*, Vol. XIX.
58 State Department memorandum, May 26, 1967, NND 969000, Box 1795, NA.
59 Ibid.
60 Ibid.
61 Report from the Israeli embassy in the United States to the Israeli Foreign Ministry, May 26, 1967, hetz 5937/30, ISA.
62 Ibid.
63 State Department memorandum, May 26, 1967, NND 969000, Box 1795, NA.

64 Ibid.
65 Ibid.

Index